LESSONS IN TEACHING
GRAMMAR
IN PRIMARY SCHOOLS

LESSONS IN TEACHING
GRAMMAR
IN PRIMARY SCHOOLS

SUZANNE HORTON AND BRANWEN BINGLE

Los Angeles | London | New Delhi
Singapore | Washington DC

Learning Matters
An imprint of SAGE Publications Ltd
1 Oliver's Yard
55 City Road
London EC1Y 1SP

SAGE Publications Inc.
2455 Teller Road
Thousand Oaks, California 91320

SAGE Publications India Pvt Ltd
B 1/I 1 Mohan Cooperative Industrial Area
Mathura Road
New Delhi 110 044

SAGE Publications Asia-Pacific Pte Ltd
3 Church Street
#10-04 Samsung Hub
Singapore 049483

Editor: Amy Thornton
Development editor: Geoff Barker
Production controller: Chris Marke
Project management: Swales & Willis Ltd,
Exeter, Devon
Marketing manager: Lorna Patkai
Cover design: Wendy Scott
Typeset by: C&M Digitals (P) Ltd, Chennai, India
Printed by: CPI Group (UK) Ltd, Croydon, CR0 4YY

Library of Congress Control Number: 2014930442

British Library Cataloguing in Publication Data

A catalogue record for this book is available from
the British Library

ISBN: 978-1-4462-8570-1
ISBN: 978-1-4462-8571-8 (pbk)

Contents

The authors

Suzanne Horton has spent 20 years working in primary schools and has had experience teaching all year groups across the primary age phase. She worked as an Advanced Skills Teacher (AST) and as a Local Authority Literacy consultant whilst maintaining a teaching responsibility in school. She is currently subject leader for primary English at the University of Worcester and teaches on a range of postgraduate and undergraduate modules. She has recently been involved in the Lifelong Readers Project in cooperation with a number of European partners, funded with support from the European Commission.

Branwen Bingle moved from primary teaching into initial teacher education in 2008. Her career path to date has been anything but straightforward: she has been a supply teacher and support assistant for Service Children's Education; a basic skills tutor working with adults in the military; a private day nursery teacher working with 3- and 4-year-olds; a secondary English teacher working across KS3 and 4, including the teaching of GCSE English; and a subject leader for English in two Worcestershire middle schools. In addition to her lecturing role, Branwen is currently working on doctoral research into children's literature and its potential influence on professional identity construction/aspiration.

Acknowledgements

Every effort has been made to trace the copyright holders and to obtain their permission for the use of copyright material. The publisher and author will gladly receive any information enabling them to rectify any error or omission in subsequent editions.

The authors would like to thank the teachers who offered advice and support along the way, in particular Suzanne Roff and Anna Michaut.

They would also like to thank their families for their unwavering support, patience and belief.

For Suzanne – Ian, Alex and Emma.

For Branwen – Keiran, Leigh-Anne, Catrin, Korbin, Callum and Mikkie.

This book would not have been possible without you.

Chapter 1

What is grammar?

Learning outcomes

The way that language is organised and structured, and how it can be utilised and manipulated to create meaning and aid communication, is a fascinating area of study in its own right. Much of the preparation for teaching deals with the skills, knowledge and understanding needed by children in order to apply these to their speech and writing; however, in order to understand truly the purpose for teaching explicit grammar skills in context, it is helpful for the teacher to have an awareness of the rich linguistic history of the English language.

This chapter will allow you to achieve the following outcomes:

- understand what grammar is and what it entails;
- understand how the historical context of the UK affected the development of grammar in the English language.

Teachers' Standards

Working through this chapter will help you meet the following standard:

3. Demonstrate good subject and curriculum knowledge.

Making sense of grammar

> When we come to literature we find that though it conforms to rules of grammar it is yet a thing of joy, it is freedom itself. The beauty of a poem is bound by strict laws, yet it transcends them. The laws are its wings, they do not keep it weighed down, they carry it to freedom. Its form is in law but its spirit is in beauty.
>
> (*Sadhana: The Realisation of Life* by Rabindranath Tagore, 1913: **https://archive.org/ stream/sdhanoounkngoog#page/n19/mode/2up**)

As the authors of this book, we make no apologies for our interest in grammar. It is not our intention to reduce it to a series of rules and laws that must be applied to all written communication, but neither do we wish to ignore the conventions of our language that enable people to manipulate texts to suit a range of audiences and purposes. Our interest comes from careers in education where we continually strive to help learners communicate, within an ever-changing educational landscape; however it is also indicative of our fascination with English language use and a love of the richness of the literature available to us using this medium.

In his book *Mother Tongue*, Bryson (1990, p2) states: *The complexities of the English language are such that even native speakers cannot always communicate effectively* and this is no truer than when discussing grammar. It has become a contentious issue, with grammarians often positioning themselves as supporters of prescriptive or descriptive approaches and dismissing the other out of hand. This discord affects the field of educational research into literacy and language: in *Teaching English, Language and Literacy* Wyse et al. (2013) describe the personal nature of some of the criticisms of studies into grammar teaching while unpicking some of the key research papers which have informed educational policy in the UK.

So why is the teaching of grammar so emotive? One of the issues, referred to above, is the debate over grammar as a prescribed set of *dos and don'ts* (prescriptive) and grammar as a description of the way speakers and writers structure and organise their language use (descriptive). The irony of a word in English being used to describe two apparently opposed ideas should not be lost on teachers often charged with explaining to pupils things such as *sanction* (to permit or to punish) or *bolt* (to run away/to fix in place); and yet this should not prevent a working definition being devised and applied in order to help children communicate effectively.

Activity

A Google search brings up some of the following information regarding grammar. Which of these statements do you agree with? Can any of them be challenged?

Grammar (noun)

1 [mass noun] the whole system and structure of a language or of languages in general, usually taken as consisting of syntax and morphology (including inflections) and sometimes also phonology and semantics.

(*Oxford Online Dictionary*, found at **www.oxforddictionaries.com/definition/english/ grammar?q=grammar**)

English-speakers use many forms of grammar. Written English tends to be more standardised.

(BBC Skillswise: English and maths for adults website, found at: **www.bbc.co.uk/skillswise/topic/varieties-of-english**)

The unit begins with an exploration of the notion of stereotypes. Students then review and extend their knowledge of grammar focusing on the use of adjectives, onomatopoeia and alliteration.

(Ofsted, 2011)

> *Not one of Ofsted's sample lessons suggests that teaching grammar explicitly is a good idea. It seems that Ofsted inspectors don't even know what grammar is, as demonstrated in the quotation above. Adjectives are grammatical features. Onomatopoeia and alliteration are not: they are stylistic devices.*
>
> (*Standpoint Magazine* (citing Ofsted, 2011) http://standpointmag.co.uk/free-at-last-june-12-inspecting-the-inspectors-katharine-birbalsingh-ofsted-michael-wilshaw-english-grammar?page=0%2C0%2C0%2C0%2C0%2C0%2C0%2C0%2C0%2C0%2C1)

- Write your own definition of what you understand grammar to include and involve. Use as many sources as you feel appropriate to help you.

The last quotation in the activity above comes from an article criticising Ofsted's subject knowledge, but if we use the *Oxford English Dictionary* definition and include phonology then alliteration seems to be a part of grammar. Thus we begin to understand why teaching grammar seems so complex: no one can agree what it is!

The historical context

The complexity of the English language is unavoidably tied up in the history of the British Isles. One of the strengths of the language is the willingness of its speakers to absorb new terms and linguistic structures, to utilise the vocabulary and syntax of other peoples in order to aid communication. This has, in turn, led to a sprawling, sometimes unwieldy language that can baffle, bemuse and often irritate scholars, while at the same time becoming a global means of communication for entertainment, business and tourism.

The original languages of mainland Britain, Celtic and Gaelic, survived the Roman onslaught but found themselves pushed ever westward by the Germanic tribes, most notably, at least in linguistic terms, the Angles (from which we derive the name of our language) and the Frisians. Old English is thus not the original medium for communication of England, but already well travelled when it joined and then dominated the landscape, providing familiar terms still in use today.

However, the runic form of representing the language did not survive so well as the spoken terms: the Romans had left their mark in many ways, not least upon the alphabetic code devised for Latin which replaced the orthography of the runes. It is merely an accident of tradition and convention that has led us to the alphabet we know today, as runic inscriptions were saved for special occasions while the Latin alphabet was utilised more prolifically and spread through the religious writings of the time; with the spread of Christianity came the spread of graphemes we recognise today. Later still the Norman invasion brought scribes who had been using alternative spellings such as 'qu' rather than 'cw', making words from different languages look as if they came from the same linguistic source. It was at this time that the grammatical structure of the language also began to change as French influenced the spoken and written mediums alongside Latin and the local vernaculars.

And herein lies the problem: the continual change brought about through invasion and expansion meant that the scribes keeping the records were often interlopers to Britain, brought along with a conquering army. It was their job to document local languages, which they did in ways recognisable to them and their readership (often a small number of scholars familiar with their alphabetic and syntactic codes). With the exploration of the globe, the scribes of the British Isles then took this abroad, bringing back new vocabulary or phraseology to describe the new places, inventions and discoveries experienced but embedded using familiar linguistic codes. This was further complicated by the rise of the printing press, when the printer and not the writer often had final say on how the text would appear in print. Local decisions regarding spelling, punctuation and syntax then had national impact, and provided the basis for many an anomaly discussed in modern classrooms. For example, William Caxton (c. 1420–1492), the man credited with bringing the printing press to England, was also the one responsible for choosing a Midlands/London dialect for the translations of the majority of the books he printed as he felt it would have wider appeal than regional dialects. He made decisions regarding spelling and grammar that affect what we read today, for example choosing between the words eggys and eyren to describe the oval object laid by birds. These decisions were not just down to personal preference: they were based on his need to print texts that would be marketable to as wide a readership as possible, as *A standard language would have been much more important to Caxton, a publisher of printed books, than to a scribe who produced one copy at a time* (**www.bl.uk/treasures/caxton/english.html**).

Until the fourteenth century the language of education had largely been that of Latin and Greek, languages with rigid and inflexible grammatical structures, especially in their classical forms. By the time of Caxton, English had finally taken over as the official and political language of the islands, although most published texts across the continent were still in Latin. The new mass production of texts in English led to the development of standardised written English and an increased opportunity for people to learn to read in English, but it wasn't until 1586 that William Bullokar wrote a *Pamphlet for Grammar*, outlining how the 'rules' of the English language should be applied to writing. Thus it was that Shakespeare had rules to break by the time he began writing in the late sixteenth/early seventeenth century!

This preoccupation with the correct and often prescribed notion of a perfect grammar which surpasses all others has continued to influence discussions about language, literacy and education. During the eighteenth century the Age of Enlightenment saw an increased number of people reading more extensively than before, and many key thinkers of the time turned their attention to linguistics. As with all areas of study this led to argument and disagreement rather than consensus, fuelled by a growing middle class that wanted to be told how they should read and write in order to join the upper echelons of society. In other words, the main reason for wanting a set of grammatical rules was to enable social mobility, as your use of language could give away your poor social standing and prevent you moving upward in social and economic terms. This argument seems to have stayed with us into the twenty-first century, as education and effective language use are continually highlighted as potential ways to break down social barriers and enable aspiration.

The idea then that there was ever a perfect time when the rules of grammar and spelling could be applied without fear of change or disagreement is erroneous when applied to English. Language has changed and adapted over time, matching the speed of technological change and global influence. Success as a communicator in a range of environments, however, relies upon your ability to use the language of that environment as effectively as possible, and thus learning the syntax, semantics, phonology and morphology of those in power, be it employers, government or educators, can lead to greater achievement than doggedly sticking to what you know works at its most basic level.

The educational context

> *In any anxiety over a contemporary situation there is likely to be a wistful look back to the past, with a conviction, often illusory, that times were better than now . . .*
>
> *Many allegations about lower standards today come from employers, who maintain that young people joining them from school cannot write grammatically, are poor spellers, and generally express themselves badly. The employers sometimes draw upon past experience for comparisons, but even where they do not there is a strong implication that at one time levels of performance were superior.*
>
> (The Bullock Report, 1975, p3)

The concern over the way grammar is taught in schools is not new. *The Bullock Report*, cited above, highlights how this is an area continually viewed as problematic; however the findings of their report point towards a need to teach children how to respond in a wide range of contexts, stating *it seems to us far more reasonable to think in terms of appropriateness than of absolute correctness (The Bullock Report*, 1975, p143). This influenced the emerging National Curriculum, which has outlined the statutory programmes of study to be taught since 1988. It has been commented upon in reports and reviews into English teaching in the UK, such as *The Kingman Report* (1988) and *The Cox Report* (1989), and more recently in Ofsted surveys and good practice reports such as *Excellence in English* (2011), and *Moving English Forward* (2012). The National Literacy Strategy, implemented in the late 1990s, detailed prescriptive and explicit grammar teaching as part of word, sentence and text-level work within a Literacy Hour; and the Primary National Strategy, although less prescriptive in approach, still made explicit the grammatical features children should be taught based on the curriculum requirements for England.

What this indicates is that grammar's place within education is indisputable: it has been a feature of English language learning since before the inception of the curriculum. So what is the issue?

To teach explicitly or not to teach explicitly? That is the question . . .

As alluded to already, much of the public debate centres on how grammar is or isn't being taught in schools. Teachers themselves often decry a lack of explicit grammar teaching from their own childhood, as if this is the reason they cannot possibly make it clear to children how to write a complex sentence or the correct use of less and fewer (it depends whether the noun is countable or not: less water, fewer cups). In *Moving English Forward*, Ofsted (2012, p41) commented on the way subject knowledge affects learning:

> *This lack of specialist subject knowledge is also likely to limit the effectiveness of some primary teachers, especially when teaching older pupils, in areas such as understanding the differences between standard and non-standard English, teaching grammar, and modelling the writing of texts such as poetry for their pupils.*

But with such little agreement on how much subject knowledge in linguistics can be expected from general specialists in primary schools, or even whether prescriptive approaches are preferable to descriptive within the classroom, this observation is at best a statement of the obvious (as a lack of subject knowledge in any aspect of the curriculum is likely to limit the effectiveness of the teaching) and at worst a smokescreen which detractors from contemporary teaching methods will use as 'evidence' that grammar teaching is not happening in school. A significant amount of the public debate ignores the use of words like 'some' when reviewing the findings of bodies like Ofsted, despite the fact that this would indicate most teachers observed had comprehensive subject knowledge in these areas.

Defining grammar

So we return to the question put forward in the opening sections of this chapter: how do you define what grammar is and, perhaps more importantly, what should be taught? It may be helpful to think of it in terms of 'pedagogical grammar', i.e. *the kind of knowledge about grammar needed by the teacher and the way this is made available to the student in the form of lessons or materials* (Derewianka, 2001, p241).

Derewianka (2001, p242) identifies four grammatical paradigms that have influenced the way grammar is taught:

1. traditional grammar;
2. structural grammar;
3. transformational generative grammar;
4. functional grammar.

She argues that pedagogical grammar should draw upon linguistic theories, while recognising the need for a more pragmatic approach when teaching.

Try to find out the basic principles for each of the paradigmatic positions.

1. How do their basic principles differ?
2. What do they have in common?

You may find it helpful to map your findings on to a Venn diagram (Figure 1.1).

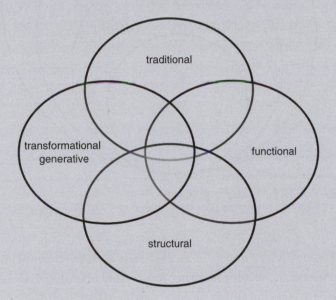

Figure 1.1 Four grammatical paradigms

While elements of structural and transformational generative grammars have influence in linguistic circles, it is more likely that traditional and functional grammars will resonate with those teaching in primary schools in the UK. Traditional grammar deals with the naming of parts and is useful from an analytical point of view as it allows the 'tools' of grammar to be labelled. From this we get the metalanguage that enables us to discuss words in sentences: nouns, verbs, adjectives, etc. Functional grammar, on the other hand, focuses on how language is used to communicate and the competence of speakers or writers in varying their use of language to suit different contexts. Within language education it is the work of Michael Halliday (b. 1925) that has most heavily influenced practice in this field through the development of Systemic Functional Grammar (SFG). Halliday's model for looking at grammar can be represented as shown in Figure 1.2.

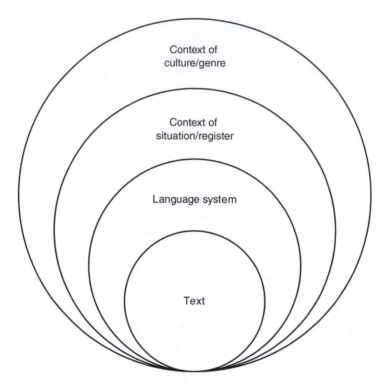

Figure 1.2 Halliday's model for looking at grammar

Within the context of situation, also known as the register, there are three variables: field, tenor and mode. In its simplest terms this deals with the *what* (field), the *who* (tenor) and the *how* (mode) of any text being constructed or analysed. Once the details of these variables are known, Halliday argues, then it will become obvious what grammatical features should be/have been utilised.

> Think about the differences in the following texts:
>
> - a letter from a parent to a child detailing the effects of a storm on the garden;
> - a newspaper article, written by a journalist, detailing the effects of a storm on a local property.
>
> Both deal with the same field (the events being described) but the tenor and mode have changed. If the parent is also the journalist then only the mode will have changed, but this will still have an impact on the type of text being produced.

Learning outcomes review

As a teacher of grammar, your role may seem unclear at times. In a blog post entitled 'PS to grammar talk', Michael Rosen wrote the following:

we (me too) all get drawn into thinking that 'real' or 'best' writing is in standard or 'correct' English. Yet, every day and night we encounter examples of moving, exciting, challenging, funny writing which is not written in this way – whether that's in drama, film, TV, song, poetry, comedy, comic strips and so on. It is an untruth to talk as if there is only one form of 'effective' English when clearly every day we are entertained by non-standard forms.

So, rather than pretending this huge body of writing and language is irrelevant and/or wrong, perhaps – in the context of talking about grammar – we should be investigating it.

(http://michaelrosenblog.blogspot.co.uk/2013/10/ps-to-grammar-talk.html)

One of the key messages from this book is that grammar should be seen in light of its use and its function within Standard English as this is the chosen dialect of education in the UK; that it only has meaning if applied to effective communication and its purpose is clear. Thus what is presented here is a starting point for ways to investigate language rather than a prescribed route through the intricacies of 'correct' grammar. By looking at grammar in context we hope to enable the development of appropriate language use across a range of text types and for a wide and varied audience.

Points to consider

- What subject knowledge do you already have about grammar?
- What elements of linguistics might benefit your teaching? Could you find out more about the work of Halliday to support your understanding of functional grammar, for example?
- At the beginning of this chapter there was a quotation from Bill Bryson's *Mother Tongue* which suggested that English was a complex language; he also states that *The richness of the English vocabulary, and the wealth of available synonyms, means that English speakers can often draw shades of distinction unavailable to non-English speakers* (Bryson, 1990, p3). How can you draw attention to and celebrate the qualities of the English language in your classroom?

Further reading

Blake, B. J. (2008) *All About Language.* Oxford: Oxford University Press.

This book combines a breakdown of the subject knowledge needed to understand the way language works with sections on the history of language and language acquisition. A useful text for teachers interested in the why and the how as well as the what.

Bragg, M. (2003) *The Adventure of English: The Biography of a Language.* London: Hodder & Stoughton.

A look at how the English language developed, and how it is ever changing to reflect who is using it and how it is being used.

Butt, D., Fahey, R., Feez, S., Spinks, S. and Yallop, C. (2001) *Using Functional Grammar: An Explorer's Guide*, 2nd edn. Sydney: NCTLER.

A step-by-step workbook through functional grammar as developed by Halliday, written with students and language teachers in mind.

Crystal, D. (2003) *English as a Global Language*, 2nd edn. Cambridge: Cambridge University Press.

A comprehensive account of the political, historical and cultural development of English languages around the world.

Crystal, D. (2010) *A Little Book of Language*. London: Yale University Press.

This is a useful and accessible text about basic linguistics, written in a way that children and adults alike can understand. It is the story of language, clearly detailing how and why English has evolved in the way it has.

Nordquist, R. Key events in the history of the English language: timelines of Old English, Middle English, and Modern English. Available at **http://grammar.about.com/od/words/a/historytimeline. htm**

Richard Nordquist, Ph.D. and Professor Emeritus of rhetoric and English at Armstrong Atlantic State University, has written a timeline of events that influenced the English language for the Grammar and Composition section of About.com.

References

Bryson, B. (1990) *Mother Tongue.* London: Penguin.

The Bullock Report (1975) *A Language for Life.* London: HMSO.

The Cox Report (1989) *English for Ages 5 to 16.* London: HMSO.

Derewianka, B. (2001) Pedagogical grammars: their role in English Language teaching, in Burns, A. and Coffin, C. (eds.) *Analysing English in a Global Context.* Abingdon: Routledge.

The Kingman Report (1988) *Report of the Committee of Inquiry into the Teaching of English Language.* London: HMSO.

Ofsted (2011) *Excellence in English.* London: Ofsted.

Ofsted (2012) *Moving English Forward: Action to Raise Standards in English* [online]. Available from: **www. ofsted.gov.uk/resources/moving-english-forward** [accessed 20 October 2013].

Wyse, D., Jones, R., Bradford, H. and Wolpert, M. (2013) *Teaching English, Language and Literacy.* Oxon: Routledge.

Chapter 2

Grammar in context

Learning outcomes

This chapter explores the pedagogical subject knowledge that underpins effective teaching of grammar and how best to address this teaching within the statutory framework introduced for September 2014. It sets out how the teaching of grammar through purposeful reading and writing opportunities will enhance the quality of the written form within the primary classroom. It discusses how knowledge of prior learning is important in planning effective lessons and how you will need to build upon previous experiences to develop writing further. By assessing individuals' needs and meeting these through personalised and contextualised learning experiences the teaching of grammar can be fun, engaging and, most importantly, effective.

This chapter will allow you to achieve the following outcomes:

- develop an overview of current debates surrounding the teaching of grammar;
- understand how teaching grammar in context will lead to better-quality writing;
- develop an understanding of the pedagogies associated with effective teaching of grammar.

Teachers' Standards

Working through this chapter will help you meet the following standards:

1. Set high expectations which inspire, motivate and challenge pupils:

    - Establish a safe and stimulating environment for pupils, rooted in mutual respect.
    - Set goals that stretch and challenge pupils of all backgrounds, abilities and dispositions.

2. Promote good progress and outcomes by pupils:

    - Be aware of pupils' capabilities and their prior knowledge, and plan teaching to build on these.
    - Demonstrate knowledge and understanding of how pupils learn and how this impacts on teaching.

3. Demonstrate good subject and curriculum knowledge:

    - Have a secure knowledge of the relevant subject(s) and curriculum areas, foster and maintain pupils' interest in the subject, and address misunderstandings.
    - Demonstrate a critical understanding of developments in the subject and curriculum areas, and promote the value of scholarship.
    - Demonstrate an understanding of and take responsibility for promoting high standards of literacy, articulacy and the correct use of Standard English, whatever the teacher's specialist subject.

Introduction

If you can tell stories, create characters, devise incidents, and have sincerity and passion, it doesn't matter a damn how you write.

(Somerset Maugham)

There appears to be considerable debate about the most effective way to teach grammar, fuelled by public discourse and current government policy. You may have views on the teaching of grammar that have been informed not only by your own experiences at school, but also by articles or books that you have read. You have only to look at the success of Lynne Truss's book, *Eats, Shoots & Leaves* (Truss, 2003) to comprehend our interest in 'bad grammar', or consider the recent publicity surrounding *For Whom the Bell Tolls* by the journalist David Marsh (2013), whose book addresses the quest for grammatical perfection. Some primary schools have even taken the step of introducing a 'zero tolerance' approach where children's spoken language reveals grammatical inconsistencies. One school recently hit the headlines for banning children from saying 'we was' instead of 'we were', because this was deemed to impact negatively upon their written work (Dixon, 2013). This led to considerable debate within the media and on social networking sites, with parents and teachers keen to articulate their views. Policy developments, academic findings and public discourse all serve to stir up the grammar debate. The politicisation of grammar together with teachers' beliefs and perceptions about how to deliver these requirements in the primary classroom can impose constraints upon effective practice. In this chapter, we will draw upon recent research which explores the most effective way of teaching grammar and also begin to reflect upon how this can be achieved within the framework of the National Curriculum for 2014.

Activity

It would be useful at this point to consider your own experiences of how you were taught grammar. What can you remember about word classes, sentence structure and the use of specific terminology? Can you think of a memorable writing activity undertaken in school? What part did grammar play in this lesson?

The great grammar debate

How should grammar be taught in schools?

Research suggests that formal teaching of grammar does not necessarily lead to improved writing standards (Hillocks, 1984; Wyse, 2001; Andrews et al., 2006). Despite this, there remains a school of thought dedicated to the idea that formal teaching of grammar should have a place within our school curriculum, something that Deborah Cameron alludes to when she states that grammar *is seen as one of those 'basics' that need to be got into children's heads sooner rather than later if they are not to be 'spoiled' for more elevated pursuits* (Cameron, 1997, p229). The book *Gwynne's Grammar* (2013) epitomises this view as the author supports a rather traditional approach to the teaching of grammar based on his own experiences, describing how the teaching of prescriptive grammar leads to a more acceptable standard of writing. He states that it is important for children to memorise grammatical rules if they are to become proficient in the writing of good English, *preferably starting before understanding is even possible* (Gwynne, 2013, p12).

The case for contextualised grammar teaching, however, has been evident in the curriculum for many years, with the *Language in the National Curriculum* training materials for teachers strongly recommending that children should have more opportunities to discuss language within meaningful contexts and *purposeful situations* (DES, 1992, p1). Furthermore, a recent large-scale study conducted by Myhill et al. (2012) concluded that discrete grammar lessons did not significantly improve writing standards: embedding the teaching of grammar within purposeful writing opportunities, where connections could be made between the concept and the effect, led to a greater improvement in the quality of writing produced, particularly where more able pupils were taught by teachers confident in their own subject knowledge.

To write effectively for a given purpose and audience, children need to have a conceptual understanding of grammar in preference to simply naming terms and features. Through a contextualised approach, children are more likely to understand how to make choices about language and employ techniques that will enhance the quality of their work. A belief that grammar should be taught through purposeful activities which allow children the opportunity to use grammar to enhance their writing lies at the heart of this book. Debra Myhill and co-authors reason that grammar teaching is most effective *when grammar input is intrinsically linked to the demands of the writing being taught* (Myhill et al., 2013, p103), thus the guidance contained in this book explores how grammar should be linked to the content of the lesson.

The National Curriculum for 2014

It would seem that grammar had been identified as a potential issue by the Education Secretary prior to the unveiling of the new curriculum for 2014 when he complained that:

> *Thousands of children – including some of our very brightest – leave school unable to compose a proper sentence, ignorant of basic grammar, incapable of writing a clear and accurate letter.*
>
> (Gove, 2010)

Michael Gove went on to promise that there would be a greater emphasis on spelling, punctuation and grammar, not only in the National Curriculum, but also in statutory tests undertaken by Year 6 pupils.

Consequently, the National Curriculum for 2014 demands that children have *a wide knowledge of vocabulary and grammar* (DfE, 2013, p15). The framework sets out what should be taught in each year group, separating learning about grammar into five sections: word level, sentence level, text level, punctuation and terminology. The first three sections outline particular grammatical concepts to be introduced during that year and the fourth section explains in detail the specific punctuation that should be taught alongside this. The final section is concerned with the grammatical terminology that children are to be taught and you will need to ensure that pupils *learn the correct grammatical terms in English and that these terms are integrated within {your} teaching* (DfE, 2013, p15). Achieving this will become clearer as you explore the chapters on effective teaching, which demonstrate how this can be successfully implemented within your lessons.

In the past, materials such as *Grammar for Writing* (DfEE, 2000) and *Developing Early Writing* (DfEE, 2001) have provided teachers with the knowledge, ideas and activities to support classroom practice together with a framework within which to work. The National Curriculum for 2014 includes a statutory appendix outlining the terminology that should be taught in each year group but as yet there is little direction as to how to deliver the grammar curriculum. However, when teaching grammatical concepts as outlined in the statutory guidance, it states that there should be *a focus on grammar within the teaching of reading, writing and speaking* and that pupils should *be encouraged to apply and explore this concept in . . . their own speech and writing* (DfE, 2013, p74). This suggests that teaching is delivered within a meaningful context rather than as discrete lessons – a key theme that resonates throughout this book. It is not sufficient to teach to the appendix, learning definitions by heart and completing grammatical exercises; children need to understand the concepts that are contained within the appendix and learn how to use language effectively to make choices as the writer and explain these choices to others.

Despite this, at the end of Year 6, pupils will be tested on their explicit knowledge of grammar, spelling and punctuation by completing exercises that may require them to identify incorrect usage; suggest alternative words; rewrite sentences with correct verb tense agreement; or match correct definitions to examples. They will also be required to apply these skills in their writing in order to demonstrate understanding of concepts within a broader context. You will need to ensure that the children in your class possess this knowledge and the ability to use it to good effect if they are to feel prepared for statutory assessments. The discussions that you have around word choice should lead to a more confident understanding of the concepts and allow children to have control over their own writing in which they understand not only the *what* but also the *how* and *why*.

Activity

Read the following examples of teaching word classes within the classroom and consider the two different approaches. Which do you think is more effective? Why? Which lesson will have the greater impact upon learning? Why?

A Year 3 class were asked to underline verbs, nouns and adjectives in a different-colour pen to represent the three word classes. When some of the children were asked about the learning, they were unsure as to why they needed to identify these particular words. Furthermore, some children were more concerned with using a ruler correctly to ensure their underlining was neat than reading the sentences to make sense of the constituent parts of the clause.

In a parallel Year 3 class, the children were watching a short video clip of *The Iron Giant*. Whilst watching the clip, the teacher asked the children to note down words to suggest how the giant moved through the trees and to record words that best described the forest scene. These were collated and discussed in terms of the effect created and displayed upon the working wall. The children were then asked to move around the classroom in role as the giant and add any other 'movement' words to the display. Only then did the teacher introduce the words adjectives and verbs and discuss how they could be used within their writing. The children went on to produce an opening scene for their own stories based on the video clip, using adjectives to describe the forest and powerful verbs to indicate how the giant moved through the trees. When asked about their learning, the children were eager to talk about their word choice and how they wanted the reader to feel upon reading the introduction to their story.

What do teachers need to know?

Teaching children about grammar and how to make effective choices as an author requires that teachers themselves are confident in their own understanding of concepts, but articles such as 'Teachers do not know enough grammar to teach new curriculum' (Payton, 2013) only serve to fuel the public debate about how grammar should be taught in schools today. Remember, it is not about teaching children the mechanics of grammar but fostering a curiosity about language, words and clauses when explored within a meaningful context.

As teachers you need to have a fundamental understanding of grammar if you are to teach writing successfully, as this will empower children to be able to use words effectively to create meaningful texts. The Teachers' Standards (DfE, 2012) state that all teachers should:

> *demonstrate an understanding of and take responsibility for promoting high standards of literacy, articulacy and the correct use of standard English, whatever the teacher's specialist subject.*

> (DfE, 2012, p7)

However, research suggests that not all teachers feel confident in their own grammatical subject knowledge or have the specialist knowledge to teach grammar in the classroom (Cameron, 1997; Hancock, 2009; Jeurissen, 2012; Watson, 2012). Furthermore, attitudes about the teaching of grammar can influence classroom practice; if your memories are of endless grammar exercises completed in silence, you may not necessarily feel excited about the prospect of expanded noun phrases. One thing is certain: as a primary school teacher, you will need to ensure that grammar is taught in the classroom and that children are prepared for statutory assessments in Year 6, as discussed in the previous section.

You may have already purchased books that define grammatical terms and explore definitions, read the statutory grammar appendix in the National Curriculum or attempted the Key Stage 2 English grammar, punctuation and spelling test. But is it enough to know the grammatical rules and the correct terminology? How does this translate into what you need to know in order to teach your class to become proficient writers and confident users of language?

Let us consider what we know already. You are able to use language on a daily basis to converse with others, construct emails, write letters and put together lesson plans, adapting your approach according to content, purpose and audience. Word choice and sentence structure will depend upon the nature of the task; for example, how you write a formal letter of complaint will look very different to a text sent to your best friend. Your implicit knowledge of grammar determines how something is written. You may not be able to articulate fully what a subordinate clause is but you have definitely used them in your writing. Similarly, children will arrive at school with an implicit knowledge of grammatical structures; they can communicate with you, with their friends, with family members; they are able to make marks on paper to create meaning. They will be using adjectives and verbs to indicate shades of meaning when engaged in conversation, but may not necessarily have the vocabulary and knowledge of terminology to verbalise what it is they are doing. How, then, do we marry this implicit knowledge with the explicit knowledge that is required within the classroom?

Pedagogical approaches to teaching grammar

A metalanguage

To ensure there is a shared understanding of the teaching of grammar and how it can be used in the context of writing, it is useful to employ a common language when talking about grammar and structure. This is known as a metalanguage – in effect, a language about language. It is a set of terms that can be used to describe and analyse the language we are using and so our quest to discover the most effective ways of teaching grammar, knowledge and understanding of grammatical terms is important. The shared language will enable you to talk confidently with the children about grammatical structures and how best they can be used to maximise the effect upon the reader. The use of a metalanguage will help to ensure there is a shared understanding of grammar and provide a way of discussing language within context using terms that everyone understands. However, knowledge of terms itself will not suffice and it is important that the use of terminology does not become the focus of the lesson to the exclusion of the purpose. Therefore, it is important that these terms are introduced to children when *exploring* and *using* language. You would not teach children to swim without introducing terms such as breast stroke, front crawl and sculling in order to communicate precise meaning and it is more than likely that you would do this whilst swimming. It is no different when teaching children about language; terms such as adverbial, subordinate clause and collective noun can all be used effectively whilst engaged in a writing activity. Thus, the use of a metalanguage will give children the tools with which to discuss choices and manipulate language confidently and purposefully.

Talk about writing

As you will have noticed, a key theme associated with the effective teaching of grammar requires discussion about language, in effect, talking about linguistic choices. Neil Mercer, in his book *Words and Minds* (2000), explains how exploratory talk is crucial if children are to make connections and that it is the teacher's role to ensure that such discussions about language choice take place. However, just because children are talking about various grammatical elements within a piece of writing, it does not mean that they necessarily understand why the text is written in a particular way. It is your job as the teacher to ensure that the links are made between terminology and the concepts you wish to introduce. Discussion is vital and questions which promote discussion and exploration of a text may include the following:

- What effect is the writer trying to create?

- How does the author make us feel sorry for that character?

- How can you convey an atmosphere of suspense in your story?

- How does this enhance the text?

- How do you feel about the ending?

- Why do you think that?

- What makes you say that . . . ?

- Which sentence sounds better? Why?

It is at this point that your own subject knowledge is important for you will need to be able to unpick some of these within the context of a piece of writing.

Example

Read the following piece of text from *The Lion, The Witch and The Wardrobe* by C. S. Lewis.

> *Above the dam there was what ought to have been a deep pool but was now, of course, a level floor of dark, green ice. And below the dam, much lower down, was more ice, but instead of being smooth this was all frozen into the foamy and wavy shapes in which the water had been rushing along at the very moment when the frost came. And where the water had been trickling and spurting through the dam, there was now a glittering wall of icicles, as if the side of the dam had been covered all over with flowers and wreaths and festoons of the purest sugar. And out in the middle, and partly on top of the dam was a funny little house shaped rather like an enormous beehive.*

Now consider what kind of atmosphere the author, C. S. Lewis, was trying to create in this passage.

The use of expanded noun phrases, such as *a glittering wall of icicles*, together with adverbial phrases, including *at the very moment when the frost came*, evokes a clear picture of the scene and puts us, as readers, in the very centre of the picture. By exploring how this enhances the text through shared reading and the modelling of writing in this style, you are able to engage children in conversations that should lead to a more comprehensive understanding of why expanded noun phrases and adverbial phrases are effective for this particular genre of writing.

Shared writing

The process of shared writing is instrumental in teaching grammar at the point of writing. It can be divided into three parts, each allowing the teacher to demonstrate effectively the skills required to compose a piece of text. The three parts are:

1. teacher demonstration, whereby you, as the expert writer, model the writing whilst verbalising your thought processes;

2. teacher scribing (whole-class composition), which requires contributions from individual pupils, usually noted down on a whiteboard, about word choice, sentence structure and layout;

3. supported composition, where your class has the responsibility of producing the next part of the text, usually working in pairs to construct sentences on whiteboards. This enables you, as the teacher, to explore the children's use of language and discuss the choices made.

Good modelling of writing with explicit teaching of grammatical structures to create particular effects will lead to confident writers – children who are willing to play with grammar and use it to good effect rather than relying on the inclusion of a number of techniques to satisfy success criteria. You need to explore writer choices and demonstrate how this has made a difference to the text and how this will create an effect on the reader. Pie Corbett (2008) refers to this as *writing as a reader*. This is a useful term to use with children as it reinforces the idea that writing is for an audience and has a purpose: two fundamental concepts when it comes to constructing texts.

Guided writing

Guided writing is the perfect opportunity to tailor your teaching to the needs of individuals as it necessitates the teaching of writing to a small group of pupils for whom you have identified a particular target. It may be that you have some children in your class who struggle to use direct speech correctly within their work and so guided writing provides the perfect opportunity for you to address this whilst your pupils are engaged in the writing process. Rather than asking pupils to complete exercises which require the addition of inverted commas to lists of sentences, you can use this time to guide them in discussing and exploring the whys and hows of using direct speech to create a particular effect with regard to composition. You are also in the best position to teach the mechanics of direct speech as it is directly relevant to the task in hand, thus ensuring the activity is purposeful and meaningful for that particular group of children.

Playing with language

The title of a recent article by Debra Myhill et al., 'Playful explicitness with grammar: a pedagogy for writers' (2013), epitomises how grammar is something to be manipulated and controlled in order to produce an effect on the reader. By knowing how to use grammar in this way, children can 'play' with texts to achieve the required outcome. Children love games and often enjoy word puzzles and problems, something that Pie Corbett builds upon in his *Jumpstart* series of books aimed at encouraging children to develop their imagination and stimulate creative thinking (Corbett, 2004). These types of quick-fire, starter activities can help to introduce grammatical concepts, assess prior learning or practise existing skills. Furthermore, they are fun, interactive and can be adapted to suit the needs of individuals and groups of children prior to embarking upon a writing activity. The lesson plans contained in this book demonstrate how the use of a starter activity can enhance your lesson and encourage children to experiment with language, making effective choices and explaining these choices to others.

A final thought

In Chapter 1, you will have explored the concept of *what is grammar?* from differing perspectives and may have begun to consider what grammar looks like within the primary classroom. This chapter is concerned with the best way in which to teach children grammar whilst satisfying the requirements of the National Curriculum. We, as the authors of this book, believe that understanding how grammar works is far more beneficial than simply transmitting information about word classes, sentence structure and the constituent parts of clauses. As Deborah Cameron states, *knowing grammar is knowing how more than knowing what* (Cameron, 1997, p236). If we advocate a more formulaic piece of writing that satisfies the need for correct Standard English, are we in danger of stifling creativity? Reducing the teaching of grammar to a set of decontextualised written exercises will not only prevent children from learning how knowledge about grammar can enhance their writing, but may also demotivate some of our potential writers. Children need to be able to control, explore, experiment with and discuss the use of grammar when writing; it is through effective teaching that these opportunities are fully explored.

Activity

Consider the following quotations. To what extent do they resonate with your own beliefs and opinions about grammar?

Effective composition involves articulating and communicating ideas, and then organising them coherently for a reader. This requires clarity, awareness of the audience, purpose and context, and an increasingly wide knowledge of vocabulary and grammar.

(National Curriculum for 2014: DfE, 2013)

It is really important that focusing on things such as spelling, punctuation, grammar and handwriting doesn't inhibit the creative flow. When I was at school there was a huge focus on copying and testing and it put me off words and stories for years.

(Michael Morpurgo)

Writing is an act of faith, not a trick of grammar.

(E. B. White)

Then suddenly, he was struck by a powerful but simple little truth, and it was this: that English grammar is governed by rules that are almost mathematical in their strictness!

(Roald Dahl)

Learning outcomes review

- Develop an overview of current debates surrounding the teaching of grammar.
- Understand how teaching grammar in context will lead to better-quality writing.
- Develop an understanding of the pedagogies associated with effective teaching of grammar.

Throughout your career in education, you will hear contrasting views on the best way to teach grammar in schools, some of which have been explored in this chapter. You should have a more comprehensive knowledge of the research associated with effective teaching of grammar and be able to consider how this impacts upon your own classroom practice. You will know how teaching elements of grammar within meaningful contexts, where you can make links between concept and effect, will produce better-quality writing as it allows pupils to make informed choices as authors in their own right.

Points to consider

- What do you consider to be the most important elements of the writing process?
- How does the ethos in your classroom support the use of grammar to enhance writing?
- How can you prepare children to become successful, independent writers who have the confidence to make, explain and defend their language choices?

Further reading

Marsh, D. (2013) *For Whom the Bell Tolls*. London: Guardian Books and Faber and Faber.

Truss, L. (2003) *Eats, Shoots & Leaves: The Zero Tolerance Approach to Punctuation*. London: Profile Books.

References

Andrews, R., Torgerson, C., Beverton, S., Freeman, A., Locke, T., Low, G., Robinson, A. and Zhu, D. (2006) The effect of grammar teaching on writing development. *British Educational Research Journal*, 32 (1): 39–55.

Cameron, D. (1997) Sparing the rod: what teachers need to know about grammar. *Changing English: Studies in Reading and Culture*, 4 (2): 229–239.

Corbett, P. (2004) *Jumpstart Literacy*. Oxon: David Fulton Publishers.

Corbett, P. (2008) *The National Strategies: Primary 'Writer-Talk'*. Available from: **www.foundationyears. org.uk/wp-content/uploads/2011/10/Writer_Talk1.pdf**

Department for Education (DfE) (2012) *Teachers' Standards: May 2012*. Available from: **https://www. education.gov.uk/publications/standard/SchoolsSO/Page1/DFE-00066-2011**

Department for Education (DfE) (2013) *The National Curriculum in England: Framework Document*. London: DfE.

Department for Education and Employment (DfEE) (2000) *Grammar for Writing*. London: DfEE.

Department for Education and Employment (DfEE) (2001) *Developing Early Writing*. London: DfEE.

Department of Education and Science (DES) (1992) *Language in the National Curriculum: Training Materials for Teachers*. Available from: **ftp://ftp.phon.ucl.ac.uk/pub/Word-Grammar/ec/linc1-12.pdf**

Dixon, H. (2013) Midlands primary school bans pupils from using Black Country dialect. Available from: **www.telegraph.co.uk/education/educationnews/10449085/Midlands-primary-school-bans-pupils-from-using-Black-Country-dialect.html**

Gove, M. (2010) All pupils will learn our island story. Available from: **www.conservatives.com/News/ Speeches/2010/10/Michael_Gove_All_pupils_will_learn_our_island_story.aspx**

Gwynne, N.M. (2013) *Gwynne's Grammar*. London: Ebury Press.

Hancock, C. (2009) How linguistics can inform the teaching of writing, in Beard, R., Myhill, D., Riley, J. and Nystrand, N. (eds.) *The Sage Handbook of Writing Development*. London: Sage Publications.

Hillocks, G. (1984) What works in teaching composition: a meta analysis of experimental treatment studies. *American Journal of Education*, 93 (1): 133–170.

Jeurissen, M. (2012) Perhaps I really didn't have as good a knowledge as I thought I had. *Australian Journal of Language and Literacy*, 35 (3): 301–316.

Lewis, C. S. (1980) *The Lion, The Witch and The Wardrobe.* London: Collins (first published 1950).

Marsh, D. (2013) *For Whom the Bell Tolls*. London: Guardian Books and Faber and Faber.

Mercer, N. (2000) *Words and Minds*. London: Routledge.

Myhill, D., Jones, S., Lines, H. and Watson, A. (2012) Re-thinking grammar: the impact of embedded grammar teaching on students' writing and students' metalinguistic understanding. *Research Papers in Education*, 27 (2): 139–166.

Myhill, D., Jones, S., Watson, A. and Lines, H. (2013) Playful explicitness with grammar: a pedagogy for writing. *Literacy*, 47 (2): 103–111.

Payton, M. (2013) Teachers do not know enough grammar to teach new curriculum. Available from: **www.telegraph.co.uk/education/educationnews/10356379/Teachers-do-not-know-enough-grammar-to-teach-new-curriculum.html**

Truss, L. (2003) *Eats, Shoots & Leaves: The Zero Tolerance Approach to Punctuation*. London: Profile Books.

Watson, A. (2012) Navigating the pit of doom: affective responses to teaching grammar. *English in Education*, 46 (1): 22–37.

Wyse, D. (2001) Grammar for writing? A critical review of empirical evidence. *British Journal of Educational Studies*, 49 (4): 411–427.

Chapter 3

Year 1: Teaching sentence demarcation

Learning outcomes

This chapter introduces the different ways of teaching sentence demarcation and how best to engage children in constructing effective sentences. It will explore the question: what is a sentence? It will also address the different types of sentences and how to use a variety of different punctuation marks to conclude a sentence.

This chapter will allow you to achieve the following outcomes:

- develop an understanding of what children need to know about sentence demarcation;
- have a greater awareness of how children learn about punctuation;
- consider engaging ways in which punctuation can be taught;
- have an understanding of some of the challenges when teaching punctuation.

Teachers' Standards

Working through this chapter will help you meet the following standards:

3. Demonstrate good subject and curriculum knowledge.
4. Plan and teach well-structured lessons.
5. Adapt teaching to respond to the strengths and needs of all pupils.
6. Make accurate and productive use of assessment.

Links to the National Curriculum

Key Stage 1 Year 1 statutory requirement

Year 1
Pupils should be taught to:

- develop their understanding of the concepts set out in English Appendix 2 by:

    ✓ leaving spaces between words
    ✓ joining words and joining clauses using and
    ✓ beginning to punctuate sentences using a capital letter and a full stop, question mark or exclamation mark

 ✓ using a capital letter for names of people, places, the days of the week, and the personal pronoun 'I'
 ✓ learning the grammar for year 1 in English Appendix 2

 • use the grammatical terminology in English Appendix 2 in discussing their writing.

(DfE, 2013)

Key focus: Using sentence demarcation

You may think of a sentence as a fundamental grammatical unit but attempting to define a sentence is a tricky matter. The *Oxford A-Z of Grammar & Punctuation* by John Seely defines a sentence as *a unit of language consisting of one or more finite clauses* (Seely, 2004, p141), whilst David Crystal asks us to *think of a sentence as a unit of language which makes sense* (Crystal, 1996, p22). The *Penguin Pocket English Dictionary* expands upon this with an official definition:

> *a grammatically self-contained speech unit that expresses an assertion, a question, a command, a wish or an exclamation and is usually shown in writing with a capital letter at the beginning and with appropriate punctuation at the end.*

(*Penguin Pocket English Dictionary*, 1987, p804)

A sentence can be simple, compound or complex depending upon the nature of the words that are included within it and this is explored in greater detail in Chapter 4. It can be made up of a single word – *Help!* – or contain more than one clause – *Although the rain had stopped play, the cricketers, who were already feeling hungry, made their way to the pavilion.* James Joyce would often write sentences that continued over a page and one of the final sentences in *Ulysses* is over 4,000 words long. However, this was a deliberate attempt to create a particular effect, as was the unpunctuated poetry of ee cummings, which specifically sought to break grammatical conventions.

Moreover, a sentence can be declarative, exclamative, imperative or interrogative. A declarative sentence conveys a statement and requires a full stop at the end. It will contain a subject and the subject will more than likely precede the verb.

> The girl ran swiftly through the darkening forest.

An exclamative sentence, as I am sure you can guess, is an exclamation, which is usually a short sentence and ends with an exclamation mark.

> Take it or leave it!

An imperative sentence is one which issues a command and often begins with a verb (in its basic form) and there is usually no subject element within the sentence. These are common when writing instructions.

> Put the book on the shelf.

Finally, a sentence that is interrogative is one that asks a question. These sentences will always end with a question mark.

> How had she managed to reach the other side of the river without a paddle?

Activity

Take a moment to categorise the following sentences, identifying whether they are declarative, exclamative, imperative or interrogative. Add the correct punctuation.

Where was everyone

Take a look at what happens next

Hold on

What had happened to the rest of the group

The restaurant had received amazing reviews

Shut up and listen

Slowly turn to face the mirror

Take the first turning on the right and then go straight on

Can sentences be sorted into more than one category?

However, the most important function of a sentence is that it makes sense to somebody else, in both its spoken form and written form. It can be more difficult to identify grammatical sentences in conversation as spoken sentences are structured differently from written sentences; what is often acceptable in spoken form would not be classed as grammatically correct in writing. For example, a child may say:

> The party was great – yeah, there were so many people, like . . . bringing presents.

If written down, the child writing the sentence would have more time to organise his or her thoughts and the sentence would probably read:

> The party was great and there were so many people bringing presents.

You need to teach awareness of sentences alongside the use of correct punctuation to demarcate sentences. It may be beneficial to explore this with children when teaching sentence construction. Choice of punctuation can considerably alter the meaning of a sentence. Take, for example, Lynne Truss's book *Eats, Shoots & Leaves*, the title of which is based on a story about a panda who walks into a bar, eats a sandwich, proceeds to shoot customers and then leaves the establishment. When questioned as to why, he suggests that the waiter take a look at a wildlife book which contains the sentence:

Panda . . . native to China. Eats, shoots and leaves.

(Truss, 2003)

The insertion of a comma after 'eats' suggests that 'shoots' and 'leaves' in this instance are verbs and not nouns, which dramatically alters the meaning of the sentence.

For the purposes of your Year 1 classroom, it may be wise to stick with an acceptable definition of a sentence whereby it usually contains a main verb, it begins with a capital letter and ends with a full stop, a question mark or an exclamation mark, and it has to feel 'complete' or make sense. However, just be aware that if a sentence does not follow these rules, it is not necessarily grammatically incorrect. Some of our greatest novelists and poets have had long and successful careers flouting these 'rules'.

How children learn about sentences

Children need to learn about sentences so that they are able to organise their writing into a comprehensible structure. You need to be able to recognise how these structures emerge and consequently, you will need to develop strategies to work with individual children to refine and improve their sentence structure. Together with sentence structure, children need to develop the skill of using punctuation effectively to convey precise meaning. As David Crystal explains:

> *Hide the punctuation and you hide the grammatical structure.*
> *And if you hide the grammatical structure, you hide the meaning*
> *of what you are trying to say.*

(Crystal, 1996, p151)

Therefore, it is unlikely that you would want to teach children to write sentences without the corresponding punctuation: the two are inextricably linked.

Children will arrive at school with an implicit knowledge of sentence structure for they will probably have been communicating in sentences for a number of years. They will have heard stories and conversations and watched TV programmes where ideas are represented in the form of sentences. They will enter Year 1 already able to express their ideas and communicate meaning. The next step is for children to be made aware of sentences in written text through reading and by eventually learning to write their own sentences. These will differ in structure from the spoken utterances which are often grammatically incorrect or do not adhere to the rules of Standard English. Build on their knowledge by drawing attention to sentences within texts and introduce the terminology as suggested in the National Curriculum Appendix 2 (DfE, 2013). Can they identify a sentence? Do they know what punctuation is needed? Are they able to distinguish between lower-case letters and capital letters? Can they already write captions and labels to communicate meaning? As a teacher, it is important that you are able to assess pupils' individual capability and build upon this by providing opportunities for all children to develop their knowledge of and ability to write sentences. The simple sentence is the fundamental grammatical structure upon which the rest of the grammar curriculum sits.

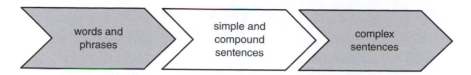

Figure 3.1 Building sentences

Teaching your class: Year 1

The lesson outlined below builds upon the learning that takes place in the Early Years Foundation Stage around clauses and sentence structure. The lesson is set outside and takes place as part of Forest Schools, as the outside environment not only can provide an alternative environment in which to learn, *it can also make subjects more vivid and interesting for pupils and enhance their understanding* (Ofsted, 2008, p7).

Your choice of text will depend upon the interests of the children and the topic that is being addressed as part of their learning. Due to the nature of this lesson and how your Year 1 sessions may be structured, you may want to adapt this lesson over a number of days.

Context

The Year 1 pupils have spent some time exploring the use of full stops and have an awareness that they conclude a sentence. The class teacher has spent some time orally rehearsing sentences so that children have a sense of a sentence as a complete thought and the children have enjoyed recording sentences on Easi-Speak microphones and talking postcards and transcribing them when constructing their own posters for the class role play area. They have also made human sentences and identified where the full stop would go. Alongside this, the Year 1 pupils have been introduced to the 'punctuation rule': a capital letter is needed for the first word of a sentence and for someone's name.

Learning objectives

- To punctuate sentences correctly using ? !
- To write sentences that make sense.

Commentary

The learning objective needs to be clearly understood by all children in the class so that they are aware of the purpose of the lesson. It is worth spending some time exploring the learning objective at the beginning of the lesson so that children understand what they need to do in order to be successful in their learning and are able to self-assess their work against

(Continued)

27

(Continued)

given success criteria, enabling them to identify what they have learnt and what they need to do next. Think about differentiated success criteria for your groups so that the learning objective is achievable yet challenging. The learning objectives above refer to the technical aspect of including punctuation at the end of a sentence and also how a sentence needs to be a complete unit of meaning if it is to make sense to others.

Starter: Punctuation detectives

Children can work in pairs or small groups to complete this activity.

All children have been asked to bring in their teddy from home to attend a teddy bears' picnic on the school field and they are sitting on the picnic blanket ready to listen to a story. However, the punctuation thieves have stolen your sentences. Can the children become punctuation detectives and find the sentences hidden on the school field?

Produce a bank of sentence strips that are differentiated according to reading ability. Sentences may include:

My ted is red.

My ted is big.

I love my teddy.

I can hug my teddy.

Group the children according to reading ability. You may want a teaching assistant or adult working in your classroom to work with a particular group to ensure that they are able to decode the sentence correctly. Cut the sentences so that they do not make sense, so for example, you may have 'My ted is' on one piece of card and 'red' on another. Encourage the children to find both parts of the sentence so that the sentence makes sense. Spend some time exploring this with individual children so that they are able to understand how a sentence should represent a complete thought. When they have collected both parts of their sentence, ask the children to discuss what might be missing from the sentence to ensure it is complete. Hopefully, the children will identify the full stop. If they are having difficulty recognising that a full stop needs to be placed at the end of the sentence, encourage individual children to look at some story books and ask them what they notice about sentences.

You will be able to assess the children's ability to recognise sentences and understand the use of full stops, which will inform your groupings when it comes to the main part of the lesson. If you have a group of children who find it difficult to recognise when a sentence makes sense, they may need some extra input around 'talking a sentence'.

Main lesson

Introduction

Read *Can't You Sleep, Little Bear?* by Martin Waddell. Explain to the children that now they have finished the teddy bears' picnic, their bears need to have a little sleep because they are tired. The children can now rock their bears to sleep or you can sing songs to help the bears go to sleep. However, the bears don't appear to want to have a sleep, rather like the bear in the story. The children need to ask their bears: *Can't you sleep, little bear?* Show the children the title of the book and ask how the sentence finishes. Discuss the use of a question mark when asking a question. How does our voice change when asking a question? Model sentences without any intonation and then repeat with a questioning tone to distinguish the difference between a statement and a question. In pairs, ask children to ask their talk partners questions about their teddy. How does their voice change?

It is important that children understand how a question is different to a statement; this can be done through exploratory talk. A study by Calkins (1980) suggested that children who talked about punctuation and how it gave meaning to text were able to use it more effectively in their own writing. Therefore it is important that you ask the children why the author has used a question mark in the title instead of a full stop. Let children talk about this and consolidate their understanding of why question marks can be used to demarcate sentences.

Explain to the children that there are some questions and statements hidden in the outside environment and they need to find them. These can then be sorted into two hoops or boxes according to whether they have found a statement or a question.

You could differentiate this activity by colour coding statements and questions and asking individuals to search for particular coloured statements and questions. This will ensure that all children are able to read the sentences; the purpose of the lesson is to understand statements and questions and it is not a decoding exercise. The children need to have a purpose for recognising how sentences are punctuated, which is achieved through the sorting activity.

Return to the teddies and settle them to sleep. The children can then formulate their own questions on mini-whiteboards, sticky notes or iPads. Maybe they could think of a question they would like to ask their teddies when they wake up, for example, What is your favourite food? Who do you like to play with? Revisit the book with the children and ask them to identify any other ways of ending sentences.

Read the sentences that include exclamation marks at the end and discuss with the children how these sentences sound. How are they different from the full stops used for statements and the question marks for questions?

It is important that you do not focus only on identifying what an exclamation mark looks like. If children are allowed to explore the reasons why exclamation marks are used in preference to full stops, they are more likely to use them effectively in their own writing. As Hall (2001, p144) explains, children need to see punctuation marks, not simply as marks which have names but as marks which have meanings. Children should have an understanding that an exclamation mark can be used in an exclamative sentence, such as 'I'm scared of the dark!' It can also be used when someone is shouting or demonstrating strong emotions, as in 'There is, out there!' when Little Bear is feeling scared about the dark.

Explain to the children that we need to wake up the teddies so that we can pack away and go back to the classroom. What could we shout in order for them to open their eyes? Take suggestions and copy these on to a mini-whiteboard or a sentence strip. Ask children to write their own sentences. Why might the sentence need an exclamation mark? Let children use this sentence to wake up their bear. Explore how the sentences we have been using today sound different according to their purpose.

Critical questions to ask pupils:

- Why do you think the author has used an exclamation mark, question mark or full stop?

- How did the author let us know that Little Bear was scared?

- Why did your voice change when asking questions?

Discuss punctuation in terms of the writing process and model the use of punctuation marks in your own writing. When embarking upon shared writing in the classroom, you need to verbalise your thought processes and make explicit your reasons for choosing specific punctuation marks. Encourage children to experiment with punctuation and read it to their partner. Does it sound right? Often, when read aloud, it will become clear where the punctuation marks should be placed in order for the text to make sense.

Practical application
Children can write their own stories about teddies going to sleep. Set up opportunities for meaningful role play in the classroom and ensure there are resources for writing questions, exclamations and statements. Use iPads, mini-video recorders or individual

microphones for children to act out their stories or record their conversations so that they can listen to the intonation in their voice.

Children will be able to apply their learning in other situations and you will need to look for examples of children using different punctuation marks and discuss this with individuals in the context of their writing. You will soon have a classroom environment in which children feel confident to experiment with the use of punctuation and use it to create particular effects to impact upon the reader.

Plenary

You could use the interactive whiteboard to show the children some sentences. Using a *Who Wants to be a Millionaire?* format and a response device (or even a show of hands if your school does not have response devices), ask the children to identify the appropriate punctuation mark that could be used. Use some sentences that are not complete so that you can explore whether they are sentences as they may not make sense. However, more importantly, ask children to read the sentence so that the use of punctuation is explored in a meaningful way.

Take this opportunity to note children who are able to identify correctly question marks, exclamation marks and full stops. Use your teaching assistant or other adults working in the classroom to sit with the children and assess the learning. If you refer to the learning objectives from the beginning of the lesson, you will know which children may need further support in subsequent lessons and be able to adapt your planning to reflect the needs of individual children.

Assessment (measuring achievement)

Assessment for learning

- Have a record of children who are using punctuation in their sentences so that you can tailor your lesson to meet individual needs. You may not need all children to look for full stops if the majority of children are using them confidently prior to your lesson.

- Use guided reading sessions to assess whether children are aware of the purpose of punctuation marks. Are they changing the way they speak when asking a question? Do they recognise speech marks and why they have been included by the author?

- Use books such as John Burningham's *Would You Rather . . .* or *Good Little Wolf* by Nadia Shireen to ask children about the punctuation and assess their understanding of how and when question marks and exclamation marks are used.

Assessment at the point of learning

- Talk to the children. Do they know how full stops work? Can they make the choice between an exclamation mark and a question mark? Can they tell you why? By talking to the children, you will gain a deeper understanding of their knowledge of punctuation and how it is used in writing.

- When children have written their statements, questions and exclamations on sticky notes, whiteboards or tablets, be aware of those children who are already using punctuation correctly. It is at this point that you can ask the more challenging questions to individuals who may need to move on in their learning. Identify your high achievers and those requiring further support.

Assessment of learning

This can be done within the classroom when you see children using punctuation successfully and applying their knowledge. It may not be as part of a formal piece of writing but when looking at children engaging in incidental writing opportunities.

- Do they orally rehearse their sentence before writing it down?

- Have they included a punctuation mark to end their sentence?

- Do sentences make sense to others?

- Are they using a variety of punctuation marks to enhance their writing?

Challenges

- Some children have a tendency to put full stops at the end of each line of writing rather than at the end of a 'complete thought'. This can often be reinforced by the books that they read in which there is one sentence on one page, therefore children do not need to take account of the punctuation. Talk to children about this and discuss books that have a number of sentences on one page, such as *The Gruffalo* by Julia Donaldson and Axel Scheffler or *Bright Stanley* by Matt Buckingham.

- You may need to explore the concept of a sentence as a 'complete thought' with some children, encouraging them to 'talk' their sentence first before committing their ideas to paper. A good idea is to record their thoughts as there will be natural pauses in their conversation which would necessitate the inclusion of a full stop if written down. Punctuation should not be seen as something to include after writing but as an integral part of the writing process. Only by understanding how punctuation marks work will you ensure that children understand how to use them correctly.

- Take care that the lesson does not become overly focused on naming the punctuation marks. Teach punctuation in the context of meaningful writing and remember that certain genres of writing lend themselves well to particular types of punctuation.

Application of learning

Links to other areas of the curriculum

The use of punctuation to mark the end of a sentence is central to all types of writing and children should be able to apply their knowledge of punctuation when attempting any form of writing across the curriculum. However, some children may find it easier to punctuate information texts or descriptive writing, particularly when it is fact-based and sentences are less complex. Make sure that you reinforce the 'rules' of punctuation in every lesson and not just your Literacy lessons.

Use PE lessons to explore *kung fu punctuation*, which can be found on the internet. A kinaesthetic approach can often help embed understanding for some groups of children.

Lessons where History or Geography are the focus can provide opportunities to model correct use of punctuation and reinforce prior learning.

Next lesson

One possible way forward is to use the information that has been gained in this lesson to inform writing in the classroom. You may want to set up an area where the teddies can 'live' for a few days and encourage children to write messages to them. These can include statements, questions and exclamations which you might want to answer from the bear's point of view once children have left the classroom!

However you choose to follow up this lesson, encourage the children in your class to take notice of punctuation and to use it effectively in their own writing to convey meaning. If they forget the punctuation in their writing, encourage them to read it back. Does it make sense? Do they need to include anything else to signify to the reader that this is a question? How can we show that someone is shouting a sentence? Or showing emotion?

Learning outcomes review

This chapter has explored how to teach a range of sentences demarcated by full stops, question marks and exclamation marks to Year 1 children. It has given some examples of how to do this with an accompanying commentary on effective teaching and learning. You should now have some ideas on how to teach punctuation in an engaging and interactive manner and will be able to incorporate this into your own classroom practice. You will know why it is important for children to learn about punctuation within the context of writing and how you can assess children in order to tailor your teaching to meet the needs of all children within your class.

Points to consider

- How might you adapt your lesson so that children can make use of the outdoor environment when you are teaching writing?
- What do you think the next steps are for your more able children?
- How will you display prompts, reminders and examples of good practice within your classroom? How can you use your working wall to support your teaching?

Further reading

Corbett, P. (2004) *Jumpstart Literacy: Games and Activities for Ages 7–14*. Abingdon: Routledge.

This book is packed with games that you can use to explore sentences. Many of the ideas can be adapted to use in all classrooms and with all learners.

Crystal, D. (1996) *Discover Grammar*. Harlow: Pearson Education.

Section 2 is particularly useful in understanding 'what is a sentence?' Activities and exercises help to consolidate understanding.

Department for Education (DfE) (2013) *The National Curriculum in England: Framework Document*. London: DfE.

Appendix 2 clearly outlines the expectations for each year group in vocabulary, punctuation and grammar. The terminology that should be introduced in each year group is included.

Truss, L. (2006) *Eats, Shoots & Leaves For Children: Why, Commas Really Do Make a Difference*. London: Profile Books.

This book can be used with children to demonstrate how the use of punctuation can alter the meaning of a sentence. There are many humorous, colourful illustrations which accompany the sentences and will appeal to children.

References

Buckingham, M. (2006) *Bright Stanley*. London: Little Tiger Press.

Burningham, J. (1999) *Would You Rather . . . ?* London: Red Fox Books.

Calkins, L. M. (1980) When children want to punctuate: basic skills belong in context. *Language Arts*, 57: 567–573.

Crystal, D. (1996) *Discover Grammar*. Harlow: Pearson Education.

Department for Education (DfE) (2013) *The National Curriculum in England: Framework Document*. London: DfE.

Donaldson, J. and Scheffler, A. (1999) *The Gruffalo*. London: Macmillan Children's Books.

Hall, N. (2001) Developing understanding of punctuation with young readers and writers, in Evans, J. (ed.) *The Writing Classroom: Aspects of Writing and the Primary Child 3–11*. London: David Fulton.

Joyce, J. (1992) *Ulysses*. St Ives: Penguin Fiction (first published 1922).

Ofsted (2008) *Learning Outside the Classroom: How Far Should You Go?* London: Ofsted.

Seely, J. (2004) *Oxford A-Z of Grammar & Punctuation*. Oxford: OUP.

Shireen, N. (2011) *Good Little Wolf*. London: Random House Children's Publishers UK.

The Penguin Pocket English Dictionary, 2nd edn (1987) London: Penguin Books.

Truss, L. (2003) *Eats, Shoots & Leaves: The Zero Tolerance Approach to Punctuation*. London: Profile Books.

Waddell, M. (1988) *Can't You Sleep, Little Bear?* London: Walker Books.

Chapter 4

Year 2: Teaching conjunctions

Learning outcomes

This chapter explores how you can teach conjunctions within the classroom. It looks at what children need to learn, what you need to know in order to teach them and how children learn.

This chapter will allow you to achieve the following outcomes:

- develop an understanding of the correct use of co-ordinating and subordinating conjunctions;
- understand the concepts of simple, compound and complex sentences;
- have a greater awareness of some of the ways in which you can teach conjunctions.

Teachers' Standards

Working through this chapter will help you meet the following standards:

3. Demonstrate good subject and curriculum knowledge.
4. Plan and teach well-structured lessons.
5. Adapt teaching to respond to the strengths and needs of all pupils.
6. Make accurate and productive use of assessment.

Links to the National Curriculum

Key Stage 1 Year 2 statutory requirement

Year 2
Pupils should be taught to:

- learn how to use:

  ✓ sentences with different forms: statement, question, exclamation, command
  ✓ subordination (using *when, if, that,* or *because*) and co-ordination (using *or, and,* or *but*)
  ✓ the grammar for year 2 in English Appendix 2
  ✓ some features of written Standard English

- use and understand the grammatical terminology in Appendix 2 in discussing their writing.

(DfE, 2013)

Key focus: Conjunctions

Children begin by learning to write simple sentences consisting of one main clause. However, through the use of conjunctions, children are able to use more sophisticated sentence constructions and join more than one clause together, thus enriching the text through the use of compound sentences and complex sentences. As children become more confident in their writing, they will be able to build upon simple sentences by using *conjunctions* to join clauses of equal importance (compound sentences) and using subordinate clauses within main clauses (complex sentences).

To teach children about the use of conjunctions, you need to understand what is meant by a clause. A clause is a group of words that represents meaning, usually containing a verb.

> The cat walked across the wall.

This is a *simple sentence* as it contains only one clause.

A sentence can consist of more than one clause and these are known as *compound sentences* and are joined by a connecting word or phrase (conjunction).

> <u>Emma ran to school</u> but <u>she still didn't make it on time</u>.

The clauses in this sentence are underlined. 'But' is the *conjunction* joining the two clauses.

A *complex sentence* also contains two or more clauses, one of which is a main clause and one of which is a subordinate (or dependent) clause.

> Although Alex had eaten all of his lunch, <u>he was still hungry</u>.

In this sentence the main clause is underlined. The clause *although Alex had eaten all of his lunch* is a subordinate clause as it does not stand alone as a simple sentence and begins with a subordinating conjunction, 'although'.

Activity

Look at the following sentences and identify whether they are simple, compound or complex sentences. Can you identify the clauses in each sentence?

I woke up early this morning.

He went to enter the building but changed his mind.

She ate her dinner quickly.

As she wandered around the garden, she noticed the birds in the trees.

She finished her drink although she did not like it.

Children will learn more about complex sentences and subordinate clauses in Key Stage 2 and so, for the purpose of this chapter, we will be focusing on the use of conjunctions to extend sentences and enrich text. Conjunctions are a type of cohesive device which connects clauses together to create longer sentences. There are two types of conjunctions: *co-ordinating conjunctions* and *subordinating conjunctions*.

The simplest conjunctions are co-ordinators which join two clauses of equal importance to form compound sentences. There are seven of these and they can be remembered using the acronym FANBOYS.

for	and	nor	but	or	yet	so

The most common of these are *and*, *but*, *so* and *or* and most children will begin extending sentences using these.

Examples:

My sister purchased the tickets *and* I bought the sweets.

Millie took her swimming costume *but* her mum had forgotten her towel.

Do you want orange juice *or* would you prefer apple?

The printer had run out of paper *so* I added more.

The other co-ordinating conjunctions are usually more difficult for children to use in their written work as they are not ones that they will regularly encounter in their own reading.

Examples:

I went to the chemist *for* I needed some medicine.

I have not entered the competition *nor* do I intend to do so.

I love broccoli *yet* I hate cauliflower.

You have only to look at the examples above to understand why some conjunctions are used more commonly than others and it is important that you teach children how to use them correctly so that their sentences make sense. For children to be able to choose the most appropriate conjunction to link two clauses they will need to hear and see them modelled correctly.

Subordinating conjunctions are used to join a subordinate clause to a main clause in a complex sentence, linking the two ideas together. For example:

I have something to eat	when	I get home from school.
main clause	*subordinating conjunction*	*subordinate clause*

They can also come at the beginning of the sentence, immediately before the subordinate clause, as in the following example:

If	you leave now,	you won't be late.
subordinating conjunction	*subordinate clause*	*main clause*

The most common subordinating conjunctions are:

| if | although | until | while | when | that | because | since |

Activity

Can you write sentences containing each of the subordinating conjunctions highlighted above? Underline the subordinate clause in one colour and underline the main clause using another colour.

How children learn about conjunctions

Most children will have learnt how to join clauses using *and* to form a compound sentence in Year 1 and may feel confident using other co-ordinating conjunctions such as *but* or *so*. They may have encountered a variety of conjunctions whilst reading independently or through shared and guided reading and, although they may not necessarily be using the correct grammatical terminology, may have an implicit understanding of how sentences can be extended in this way. To extend their learning, you need to teach children about alternative conjunctions to avoid text that is either overly reliant on short sentences to convey information or simply populated throughout with the conjunction *and*. Introduce children to the term *conjunction*, although make sure that this is done in context rather than introducing the term as an abstract concept. Children often enjoy learning these technical terms but it is necessary that they know what they are and how to use them if they are to move on successfully in their learning. There are a number of excellent children's books that use a variety of conjunctions which may be help to familiarise children with this grammatical convention. These include *My Brother* by Anthony Browne, *Just Me and 6,000 Rats* by Rick Walton and *Who's Afraid of the Big Bad Book?* by Lauren Child.

Work with individual children when writing, and guide them to extend their sentences using *but*, *or*, *yet* and *so*. Ensure that you give children sufficient opportunities to rehearse their sentences orally before writing so as to consolidate understanding. Once children have become familiar with, and confident in, the use of co-ordinating conjunctions to join clauses, introduce the use of subordinating conjunctions to vary sentence structure. However, it is important that we do not put a ceiling on children's learning and that you teach children according to their ability and need rather than following a checklist of concepts devised for a particular year group.

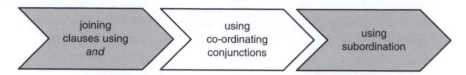

Figure 4.1 Learning conjunctions

Teaching your class: Year 2

The lesson outlined below demonstrates one way in which you can teach a Year 2 class about co-ordinating conjunctions. The commentary explains the thinking behind the teaching and will help to explain the pedagogies associated with the teaching of grammar. However, you will need to consider the needs and interests of your class. We suggest some useful resources that would help teach conjunctions but you will also have your own ideas based on your knowledge of the children in your class.

Context

The children in Year 2 have been reading books by Jez Alborough (including: *It's the Bear*, *My Friend Bear* and *Where's My Teddy?*), acting out various scenarios during role play activities and discussing the characters and their actions. They have looked at diary extracts and discussed features of recounts, most notably:

- chronological order;
- past tense;
- first or third person;
- time connectives.

They have been encouraged to bring in a favourite teddy or figure from home and talk about what it might get up to when they are at school. They have recorded their ideas as a talking diary, acting in role, using the first person, and these have formed part of a classroom display based around time connectives. To extend their use of co-ordinating conjunctions in order to lengthen sentences to include more detail, the children have been asked to produce a storyboard outlining teddy's day. This will lead to the children using video equipment or iPads to produce a short film of teddy's adventures, culminating in a screening of the films and a mock Oscar ceremony. This ensures that the children have a purpose and an audience for their writing. Because the children will have to plan teddy's day, they will need to illustrate and write a number of sentences explaining what is happening. They will have to explore the use of conjunctions to join clauses so as to create interest for their chosen audience.

Learning objectives

- To be able to identify co-ordinating conjunctions.

- To use co-ordinating conjunctions correctly to join clauses.

- To know that co-ordinating conjunctions allow the writer to add more detail within a single sentence.

Commentary

It is important that children understand what they are learning and why. This is echoed in Jackie Beere's book, *The Perfect Ofsted Lesson*, where she explains that pupils need to see how this lesson sits within the wider framework of their learning. You will undoubtedly be familiar with the idea of displaying the learning objective within the classroom but, as Jackie Beere goes on to state, it is not enough to write them down: you need to ensure that the students have engaged with them and can explain them to an observer (Beere, 2010, p51).

The learning objectives for this lesson identify three important skills in learning about co-ordinating conjunctions: identifying them, using them and knowing why they are used. If children cannot identify a conjunction within the context of a sentence, they will probably be unable to use one effectively. Unless they can use conjunctions accurately, they will probably be unable to explain why they have used one. The more you talk about how conjunctions are used to extend sentences and add detail to texts, the more they will become an automatic addition within texts.

Starter: Conjunction construction

Organise the children into mixed-ability groups of no more than four and hand each group a bag containing some small world play figures and flashcards of co-ordinating conjunctions. Activate an online timer and then ask the children to arrange the small world figures into a scene and suggest a sentence using the conjunction contained in their bag to describe what is happening. For example, they may arrange a selection of Lego people and cars so that the cars are unable to continue driving down the road. The sentence may be:

> The driver needed to get home *but* there was a traffic jam.

Or:

> The driver didn't know if he should stop *or* turn round.

Commentary

Immediately, the children will start to talk about the various scenarios that can be created using the small world play figures and will have to discuss and refine their ideas accordingly. They will be extending their vocabulary and because they have to incorporate a conjunction in order to form a compound sentence, they will have to structure their sentence correctly to reflect this. If you wish to differentiate this activity, think about how you share out the flashcards containing conjunctions: some, such as 'yet' and 'so', are trickier to incorporate into a sentence and may be more suited to a group of children with a more varied language vocabulary. If you have some children in your class requiring more support with sentence construction, you could have a collection of words in the bag which they need to rearrange in order to construct a sentence. Adapt the starter to suit the needs of your class.

During this activity, extend children's thoughts and encourage them to rehearse their ideas orally. Does it sound right? Could they use an alternative conjunction? How does this change the meaning of the sentence? You are already beginning to assess the children in your class and you should be able to group them in a more meaningful way when it comes to supporting them during independent work.

Main lesson

Introduction

Set the context of the lesson by explaining that they are to produce storyboards of 'a day in the life of teddy' which will reflect what teddy does when they are at school. Explain the purpose of the activity and the required outcome. Share the learning objectives and check understanding by questioning appropriately.

Begin by showing the children a slide show of the class teddy's day. If you don't have a class teddy, introduce them to your teddy and tell them a little bit about what he likes to do. If teddies don't work with your class, you may want to use popular children's figures or a class pet instead. Sequence the slide show so that we see teddy playing in the garden, eating lunch in the kitchen or going shopping (you will have had to take photographs prior to this lesson in order to develop the slide show, so be prepared for some strange looks in the supermarket!). Ask the children to tell a partner what is happening in each of the pictures and predict what might happen next; the only requirement is that the sentence contains a conjunction. They can use mini-whiteboards or recording devices to record ideas. You could act as a scribe for some children. Make a note of any interesting sentences on the whiteboard or ask a teaching assistant to note ideas on sticky notes. Choose three to four sentences and write them on the interactive whiteboard or on an easel. Ask children to read them aloud, adding actions as they speak.

Commentary

You will need to assess the interests of your class for this particular lesson and choose a class teddy or pet to write about that will provide a meaningful context. By talking about teddy's day, children are automatically using features of a recount and will be using the third person, past tense and time connectives. You need to encourage all children to formulate sentences containing conjunctions and so it may be relevant to display them on the working wall or as prompts on the table. Be aware of children who may not necessarily have the transcriptional skills to write sentences on the mini-whiteboards and employ the use of recording devices such as Easi-Speak microphones or talking postcards. Not only will this ensure that children can articulate sentences, it can act as a suitable motivator when it comes to writing sentences at a later date.

Once three to four sentences have been chosen to illustrate Ted's day suitably, write them on the interactive whiteboard, remembering to verbalise your thought processes and justify your word choice as you write. Your sentences may look a little like this:

Ted wondered if he should wear the red shorts or his blue shorts today.

Ted went into the garden but it was raining.

Ted went to the top of the climbing frame so he could see the rest of the park.

(Continued)

(Continued)

You may be familiar with Pie Corbett's Talk for Writing materials which advocate oral storytelling as a way of embedding story structure and building up a bank of narrative structures. He explains how memorising stories through hearing them and joining in with them helps children to internalise language patterns so that they are able to call upon these structures when composing their own stories (Corbett, 2006). Read aloud with the class the three sentences above using actions to represent Ted putting on shorts, going into the garden, seeing the rain, climbing. Once these actions have been established and rehearsed, introduce actions for the conjunctions, for example, hand on your head for 'but', or waving your hand from side to side for 'or'. You may want to refer to Pie Corbett's *Bumper Book of Storytelling into Writing* (Corbett, 2006), for alternative actions. The purpose behind this is for children to become very familiar with the use of conjunctions in sentences by saying them aloud - much more effective than underlining them in lists of sentences. They are using them and, more importantly, using them in context.

Critical questions to ask pupils:

- Identify the co-ordinating conjunction.

- What information is contained within this sentence?

- Could you use an alternative conjunction? Would it still convey the same meaning?

- Can you move the co-ordinating conjunction to a different place within the sentence?

Practical application

Children can work in pairs or small groups to draw three to four pictures of their teddy's day. This could be completed outside of the Literacy lesson so that you are able to concentrate on use of conjunctions within a text. Alternatively, you might use this part of the activity as further oral rehearsal and consolidation of sentence structure. Ask the children to formulate sentences for each part of the storyboard, using a conjunction to join the clauses so that one sentence contains more than one piece of information. Identify the level of support that may be required for each individual and provide appropriate scaffolds in the form of prompts, sentence starters and vocabulary lists. You may choose to work with a group to explore misconceptions and misunderstandings. Remember to address the needs of your more able writers by including a suitable element of challenge. For example, introduce them to subordinating conjunctions and demonstrate how they can be situated within a sentence. Encourage children to use expanded noun phrases and adverbs to describe how Ted feels and explore how conjunctions may be used in more complex sentences. Extend children's thinking by asking questions that encourage them to justify inclusion of a particular conjunction. Why have you used ***but** it began* *to pour with rain* instead of ***and it began to rain***? Can you think of a time when we might use the conjunction *yet*? What does it mean? Can you find examples in books that you have read?

Commentary

This part of the lesson could be included in an extended writing session and will require children to use their knowledge of conjunctions to join sentences and encourage them to add detail to their writing and communicate their ideas effectively. They will be applying their knowledge of clauses, compound sentences, conjunctions and sentence construction so that they are able to write more sophisticated sentences. The requirement of a storyboard upon which they can base their film ensures a purpose for their work and, through the use of conjunctions to extend sentences, children are able to acknowledge that they can convey detailed information in a more cohesive manner.

Plenary

Refer to the learning objectives from the beginning of the lesson. Give each child a bookmark with the three objectives printed on one side. Encourage every child to self-assess against each of the objectives by marking the statements with a symbol indicating their confidence against the objectives. You may choose to use smiley faces or a traffic light system to indicate degrees of success.

Commentary

Once you have collected these from the children, you will be able to assess the learning and group children with similar levels of confidence in subsequent lessons. If children are able to refer to these bookmarks for the duration of the lessons on conjunctions, they will be able to see how their knowledge and confidence have grown, thus situating their learning within a wider framework.

Assessment (measuring achievement)

Assessment for learning

- During the starter activity, you will have the opportunity to assess the pupils in your class against the lesson's objectives so as to ensure that the learning for each child starts at the point of need, leading to personalised learning. Not all children will begin at the same starting point in their knowledge of conjunctions. Some may have had extensive reading experience; some may have a wide and varied vocabulary. It is important that you plan for this and adapt your lesson to suit the needs of the individuals. Assessment is an integral part of your lesson and should be used to shape your teaching.

- As the lesson progresses, note children who are using conjunctions effectively in their work and listen in to their discussions to assess who can identify conjunctions correctly. Use this information to challenge and extend learning by asking children to explain why they have used a particular conjunction to join two clauses. Suggest alternative conjunctions so that children have to think about sentence construction.

Assessment at the point of learning

- You may want to introduce a mini-plenary to assess learning during the lesson. Ask children to identify conjunctions they have used in their work. Can they write them on sticky notes to add to the working wall? Ask children to discuss their choice with a talking partner in order to clarify meaning and understanding.

- If you have made the decision to work with a guided group, be clear as to your focus and how you will know if each child has fulfilled the learning objective. Use questions to assess understanding; for example, which would be the better conjunction? How can we add some more information to this sentence? If children are identifying correct conjunctions, it is likely that they understand their function within a sentence.

Assessment of learning

- What evidence is there that each child has achieved and moved forward in their understanding of conjunctions? Not all children will progress at exactly the same rate, therefore it is important that you have taken into account their starting point in order to assess learning. Look carefully at the bookmarks you have collected which indicate confidence and understanding from each child's perspective. Does their self-assessment correspond with your knowledge of each child? Is it reflected in their written work?

- Because the children are working as part of a pair or group, you will need to look carefully at their contributions during independent work in order to assess learning. Make notes during sessions to indicate those children who have achieved the learning objective. You may find it useful to annotate your planning sheets to reflect achievements and inform future planning, taking into account each child's ability.

Challenges

- Take care not to rely too heavily on a narrow list of co-ordinating conjunctions. If a child wants to use subordinating conjunctions such as *since* or *until*, encourage this by exploring it in context. Use the word in sentences, model it and add to your working wall so that other children can see how it works within a sentence.

- Some pupils benefit from the support of a visual or auditory prompt, particularly children for whom English is an additional language and children who may require a multi-sensory approach. In his book *Writing Exciting Sentences*, Alan Peat (2008) suggests we remind children to use the conjunctions *but*, *or*, *yet* and *so*, using the acronym BOYS. Asking the children to include a BOYS sentence can remind them to extend sentences but they need to be aware of why they are using that particular conjunction and how it shapes the rest of the text. Exposure to story books such as the ones identified earlier in this chapter gives children opportunities to explore these sentence structures in context. Asking them to include a BOYS sentence can be a useful prompt for some groups.

Application of learning

Links to other areas of the curriculum

Conjunctions are used to extend sentences and convey information. This information will depend upon the choice of conjunction. When we use *and*, we are indicating that there is further detail or clarification included in the sentence. *Or* indicates an alternative and *but* signifies a contrast in meaning. Because of their function, sentences containing conjunctions are a natural inclusion when constructing texts in all genres and subjects. The lesson outlined above is relevant when teaching Year 2 children to use conjunctions to extend simple sentences in order to form compound sentences. As children extend this work to include subordination, they need to ensure that they write with this level of sophistication within all curriculum areas. The use of conjunctions to improve sentence construction and text cohesion could also be explored in the following ways:

- Science: When a report requires an element of cause and effect, children will need to use conjunctions such as *and*, *but*, *or*, *yet*, and *so* to convey exactly what happened and why.

- History: As we have seen from the suggested lesson plan, conjunctions feature strongly in recounts, therefore it may be beneficial to highlight them when writing about aspects of History. Read some of the *Horrible Histories* books by Terry Deary to examine conjunctions using cross-curricular texts.

- Design and Technology: Constructing plans and evaluating processes will enable children to use their knowledge of conjunctions.

Next lesson

Following on from the lesson outlined above, use the storyboards to illustrate particularly good examples of compound and complex sentences. Model using these to create a cohesive paragraph in which writing flows due to the nature of the sentence structure. Contrast this with a paragraph which contains a number of simple sentences, emphasising its repetitive nature. Read the two paragraphs and allow children to gain a sense of how the text sounds. By reading aloud, children will continue to internalise those sentence structures that lead to a more sophisticated style of writing.

For children having difficulty using subordinating conjunctions, cut up sentences on large pieces of card and encourage them to reconstruct the sentences, changing the position of the words to best effect. This will enable children to understand how we can use words to indicate precise meaning. The opportunity to move words around physically can be less daunting than committing a sentence to paper.

Learning outcomes review

You should now have an understanding of the correct use of subordinating and co-ordinating conjunctions and how these are used to extend simple sentences to create either compound or complex sentences. You should also have ideas for ways of working with children when teaching conjunctions and the importance of sentence structure to form a cohesive paragraph. In addition, you should be more confident in assessing pupils' use of conjunctions and formulating next steps in their learning.

This lesson plan provides one example of how to teach conjunctions within the context of a Literacy lesson and its fundamental structure may be applied when teaching other elements of grammar. It can be easily adapted to accommodate the needs of your class and can act as a starting point for exploring conjunctions in a meaningful and purposeful manner.

Points to consider

- How might you build upon this work to explore subordination within complex sentences?
- What provision will you make for children in your class with special educational needs?
- How might you use the storytelling techniques when teaching other aspects of grammar?

Further reading

Corbett, P. (2006) *The Bumper Book of Storytelling into Writing Key Stage 1*. Wiltshire: Clown Publishing.

This is a comprehensive collection of stories to use as a storehouse of ideas for children in Key Stage 1. There is also a similar book for Key Stage 2. It supports the teaching of language structure and patterns.

Department for Education and Employment (DfEE) (2001) *Developing Early Writing*. London: DfEE.

Although no longer available to order, you can download it from various websites. There is some useful information and practical ideas on teaching conjunctions in Unit 10, entitled At the Seaside.

http://literacyresourcesandideas.edublogs.org/2013/06/18/new-fiction-texts-that-teach/

This link provides lists of children's books that are particularly useful when teaching different genres. It also suggests books to use when teaching particular grammatical concepts.

Peat, A. (2008) *Writing Exciting Sentences*. Stoke: Creative Educational Press.

www.alanpeat.com/resources/BOYS.html

This book and corresponding website provide a number of prompts and ideas encouraging children to include a variety of sentence types in their writing.

References

Alborough, J. (1992) *Where's My Teddy?* London: Walker Books.

Alborough, J. (1994) *It's the Bear*. London: Walker Books.

Alborough, J. (1998) *My Friend Bear*. London: Walker Books.

Beere, J. (2010) *The Perfect Ofsted Lesson*. Wales: Crown House Publishing.

Browne, A. (2007) *My Brother*. London: Random House Children's Publishers UK.

Child, L. (2002) *Who's Afraid of the Big Bad Book?* New York: Hodder Children's Books.

Corbett, P. (2006) *The Bumper Book of Storytelling into Writing Key Stage 1*. Wiltshire: Clown Publishing.

Deary, T. (1993–2013) *Horrible Histories* series. London: Scholastic.

Department for Education (DfE) (2013) *The National Curriculum in England: Framework Document*. London: DfE.

Peat, A. (2008) *Writing Exciting Sentences*. Stoke: Creative Educational Press.

Walton, R. (2007) *Just Me and 6,000 Rats*. Utah: Gibbs Smith.

Chapter 5

Year 3: Teaching direct speech

Learning outcomes

This chapter explores how to teach direct speech. It explores what children need to learn, what you need to know in order to teach them and how children can use it to enhance their writing.

This chapter will allow you to achieve the following outcomes:

- develop an understanding of how direct speech is used to define character in narrative;
- develop understanding of the use of direct speech to enhance writing;
- know how to use speech punctuation correctly;
- become more confident when teaching direct speech.

Teachers' Standards

Working through this chapter will help you meet the following standards:

3. Demonstrate good subject and curriculum knowledge.
4. Plan and teach well-structured lessons.
5. Adapt teaching to respond to the strengths and needs of all pupils.
6. Make accurate and productive use of assessment.

Links to the National Curriculum

Lower Key Stage 2 statutory requirement

Years 3 and 4
Pupils should be taught to:

- indicate grammatical and other features by:

  ✓ using and punctuating direct speech

- use and understand the grammatical terminology in Appendix 2 accurately and appropriately when discussing their writing and reading.

(DfE, 2013)

Key focus: Using direct speech

Use of direct speech is particularly effective in narrative writing. The inclusion of direct speech in a story can convey the mood and personalities of the characters, bringing them to life in the mind of the reader. Through a character's voice we can determine his or her mood or emotional state: is the person angry, content, surprised or miserable? By using direct speech, as a writer, a child can capture the reader's interest, building tension or excitement within the narrative.

In order to write effectively, children need an understanding of how using speech can enhance their work and define character. They also need to know how to use the conventions of speech punctuation correctly so that the reader knows who is speaking and when. When teaching direct speech you need not only to understand these rules, but also how to teach them in an effective and engaging manner so that it does not become an abstract exercise. The prime function of direct speech is to enhance writing and contribute to the tone and atmosphere of the story. There is a tendency for some children, once they have learnt how to include direct speech, to produce sentence after sentence of speech, which only serves to make the writing stilted. By teaching direct speech in context, children will begin to make the connection between the how and why, and will use it to enhance the text rather than just because they can.

Direct speech is a sentence or a number of sentences constructed so as to convey a message within the text and can provide further meaning through the use of the vocabulary used. It can convey meaning, tone and atmosphere through the use of accompanying verbs or adverbs. In the following example, the first sentence does not give any clues as to how the character feels in a particular situation. However, through the inclusion of a *powerful* verb or an adverb, you are able to gain a sense of how the character feels, as illustrated in the second and third sentence:

'Where are you?'

'Where are you?' whispered Sam.

'Where are you?' Sam cried desperately.

To teach direct speech effectively, you will need to ensure that children are aware of the rules and conventions of speech punctuation. Where do you put the speech marks? Do you need a comma? When do you start a new line? It is important to remember that direct speech must be separate from the rest of the text and that the reader should know who is speaking. If children are aware of this, it helps to make sense of why they should include it in their narrative writing.

- The spoken part of the text must begin and end with inverted commas. Do not include anything within the inverted commas which is not either part of the speech or the associated punctuation.

- All punctuation which is part of the speech must be included within the inverted commas. For example:

   'How did you get here?' not 'How did you get here'?

- Every time a new speaker says something, you should start a new line. For example:

   The sun shone brightly that morning as the two children walked towards the house. 'Where are you going after lunch?' Sam asked.

   'I'm off to the beach,' replied his sister as she started to run down the path.

   'Only when you have finished tidying your room!' called their mother.

- If direct speech comes after the reporting clause you will need to use a comma to introduce the piece of speech, placed before the first inverted comma. For example:

   Jamal replied, 'It's in the cupboard.'

- If the reporting clause comes after a statement then a comma should be used in place of a full stop. If the speech contains an exclamation or a question then the appropriate punctuation mark should be used:

   'Mum has given me lettuce sandwiches again,' she sighed.

   'Stop thief!' yelled the shop-keeper.

   'Where are my football boots?' queried Aaliyah.

- If the direct speech is broken up by the reporting clause, you need a comma (or a question mark or exclamation mark) to end the first piece of speech and a full stop or another comma before the second piece of speech begins. For example:

   'There's no going back,' he shouted. 'We have to do it.'

   'Keep back!' he cried. 'It's too dangerous!'

Activity

Choose a short piece of fiction text containing speech which you would consider using with a Year 3 class. In order to illustrate the rules outlined above, highlight particular sections of text that you could use to model the conventions of direct speech.

If possible, try your ideas out with a group of children and then review and adapt as necessary for use in a future lesson.

How children learn about direct speech

Children should already be familiar with the concept of direct speech as they will probably have encountered some form of speech in books that they have shared in school and at home. In addition, there is often an element of speech in reading scheme books which many children read in school. They will almost certainly be able to recognise when a character is speaking and more than likely reflect this in their expression when reading aloud. However, they may not necessarily fully understand the conventions of direct speech or be able to use it effectively to enhance their writing. Once children are familiar with using direct speech to signify a character is speaking, there is often a tendency to include pages of direct speech with little else in between, which causes the text to become stilted and slow. Direct speech needs to be interspersed with description and action in order to move the story forward. Therefore the next stage is to be able to use direct speech to indicate personality, mood, tone and atmosphere within a text.

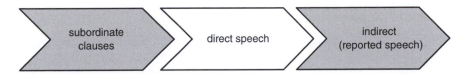

Figure 5.1 Learning about direct and indirect speech

Through the use of shared writing, you will be able to model how to write direct speech correctly, using commas, speech marks, exclamation marks and question marks to punctuate the text. Furthermore, shared writing will provide you with opportunities to demonstrate how using speech can convey a character's personality or motives through the choice of associated adverbials and verbs. Does your character need to shout or whisper? Is the character saying the words angrily or despondently? Word choice as well as punctuation will have an effect on the reader and both are part of the process of learning about direct speech.

Teaching your class: Year 3

The following lesson illustrates one way in which you can teach children about direct speech within the context of a Literacy lesson. The rules for writing direct speech remain the same however it is taught, but remember to make the lesson purposeful and relevant to your class in order to provide a contextualised approach to teaching grammar. Consider how you might use a cross-curricular approach to ensure application of skills in other areas.

Context

This Year 3 class have been reading the book *The Great Kapok Tree* by Lynne Cherry as part of their rainforest theme. They have already explored a number of non-fiction texts to gather facts and information to contribute to their own leaflets and persuasive posters. They have discussed the moral and ethical dilemmas associated with rainforests and researched the Amazon rainforest as part of their ongoing topic. The class have visited the local botanical gardens and a speaker from a local ecology group has provided further information. To ensure that pupils have something to say in their narratives and understand how a character feels and acts, several drama strategies may be used to provide pupils with a convenient vehicle through which to convey speech; this can be recorded in their own narratives using the written conventions of speech. Because speech can be incorporated into most narratives, you can adapt this lesson to reflect the topic that underpins your teaching for that year group. For example, you may be finding out about a particular period in history or exploring the life of a famous person. When children are writing a story about this, they will more than likely need to include some form of conversation in order to distinguish it from a biography or other form of literary non-fiction.

Learning objectives

- To be able to use punctuation in direct speech correctly.

- To be able to choose appropriate verbs and adverbials to describe how the character is speaking.

- To use dialogue effectively to convey meaning.

Commentary

The first step in providing formative assessment in the classroom is through the sharing of the learning objective (Clarke, 2001). You should always share the learning objectives with the children as this will enable them to focus on what it is they are learning rather than on the activity. It also allows pupils to take responsibility for their own learning and provides a framework within which to measure their success. The learning objectives for this lesson emphasise how using direct speech correctly will ensure that the quality of the writing is enhanced through dialogue that enriches the text, providing the reader with an insight into the character's thoughts and contributing to the meaning of the story. Discuss what this might look like and how the children can assess their work against success criteria.

Starter: Conscience alley

Ask the children to sit facing each other in two lines, each with a strip of sugar paper and a felt pen. Briefly recap on the story of *The Great Kapok Tree* and ask children in one of the lines to act as the woodcutter's employers and the children in the other line to take on the role of one of the rainforest animals. They must decide what they would say to the woodcutter so as to persuade him whether or not to cut down the trees. Explain to the children that they are to take part in a 'Conscience Alley'. As the woodcutter, you will walk through the middle of both lines whilst one by one the children give their reasons for and against cutting down the trees. When you reach the end of the lines, you can make your decision.

For example:

> You won't get paid if you do not finish the job. (Employer)

Or

> Where will we live if you cut down the trees? (Snake)

Then ask the children to write what they have said on the piece of coloured paper, using speech punctuation.

Commentary

If you ask children to verbalise their thoughts through a drama activity, they will be able to recognise that their thoughts have become speech. You may want to ask the children to discuss their reason with a talk partner prior to beginning the 'Conscience Alley', especially if there are some children who have difficulty taking on a role: this will depend upon your class and how familiar they are with acting in character or role play. Through observing their written sentence, you will be able to identify those children who can quite easily use correct speech punctuation but may not use appropriate adverbs or those children who are unsure as to where to include commas and exclamation marks. By using the starter as a meaningful assessment for learning activity, you will be able to group the children according to individual need and ensure that you are teaching grammar effectively.

Main lesson

Having established groups for the main teaching session, explain that they are going to continue to write the next part of the rainforest story. To ensure children have a purpose for their writing you may want to tell them that you have misplaced your copy of *The Great Kapok Tree* or that the last few pages are damaged and you were due to read this story to the children in Reception or Year 1. Tell the children that they are going to write the end of the story so that you don't have to disappoint the younger children.

Commentary

It is quite difficult to set up a real-life context for writing speech as it is not a convention we use in writing on an everyday basis: speech tends to be included in fiction and children are usually more motivated when they have a sense of audience and purpose. Rather than simply writing it for the teacher, their story will be read to other children. This should motivate the children to think carefully about their use of grammar to enhance the text and you can emphasise the need for correct punctuation as this will determine how the story will be read.

Model writing the opening sentences of the next part of the story on the interactive whiteboard so as to ensure that all children are familiar with the use of direct speech and how to punctuate this correctly. Children can use mini-whiteboards or classroom tablets to write suggestions for dialogue that would be appropriate for the story. Use this time to assess whether the children are using punctuation correctly and address any misconceptions.

Commentary

Shared writing is a term that describes the whole class writing together and is comprised of three distinct parts which will allow you explicitly to model effective strategies that children can employ in their own writing. The three stages are as follows:

1. Teacher demonstration. This is where you model writing the first few sentences as the 'expert writer' whilst verbalising your thoughts, processes and grammar choices. In effect, you are telling the children what you are doing but, more importantly, why.

    For example, you may write the sentence:

    'Please, please don't destroy our homes,' the snake begged. 'Where will we live?'

At this point, you will need to draw attention to your use of repetition with the word 'please' to indicate that the animal is pleading with the woodcutter. You have chosen the verb 'begged' as it suggests that the animals are in a desperate situation and is far more powerful than the word 'said'. In addition, show the children that you are enclosing only the spoken words in inverted commas to indicate speech but closing them after the relevant punctuation is used. Remember, you will need to add a comma before the reporting clause ('the snake begged'). Draw attention to the fact that you are placing the question mark within the inverted commas.

2. Teacher scribing (whole-class composition). The children become more involved in the composition, using their mini-whiteboards, sticky notes or tablets to write down their suggestions. You may want to encourage the children to discuss this with their 'talk partners' first so that they can verbalise their thoughts and refine their ideas. Building upon the teacher demonstration, ask children for contributions. For example, how do you think the woodcutter would say this? Can you note down an appropriate adverb to describe how he is speaking? Can you think of a question that the woodcutter may ask? You now need to choose the contribution that you are intending to include and explain your reasons for this choice, once again reinforcing the teaching points around the use of direct speech.

3. Supported composition. The focus is upon children's composition and provides an ideal opportunity for you to make continued assessments as to who may need support in subsequent lessons and identify those children who may need a further challenge. At this point, you might ask the children to work in pairs to write down the woodcutter's reply whilst thinking carefully about how they would punctuate the sentence. As they show you their contributions, you may want to challenge the more able by asking them to think of an adverb to describe how the woodcutter is speaking. You could also differentiate by asking some children to write a sentence that has a reporting clause in the middle or suggest that they include specific punctuation such as exclamation marks or question marks. This will ensure that you are addressing the differing abilities within your class.

If children are not shown the processes that writers go through in order to commit their thoughts to paper, they will not necessarily understand how they can improve their own writing. You will need to verbalise your thoughts and make your word and grammar choices explicit. Teachers do not always find this easy (Ings, 2009; Ofsted, 2009); therefore you will need to plan in advance the sentences you intend to model during this process to ensure that you are teaching the children effective strategies that they can build into their own writing.

Practical application

Children can write the ending to the story using effective dialogue to add meaning to the text. Remind them of the learning objectives and ensure that you have provided scaffolds such as writing frames, microphones, prompts and examples of speech to ensure that all children can achieve. During the starter activity and the shared writing you will have identified those children requiring further support when using direct speech and these may form a guided group. What about those children for whom direct speech poses no difficulties? An effective way in which to continue to develop their use of direct speech is to place envelopes on their tables with a further challenge included. For example, ask them to include a conversation between three characters or try splitting the direct speech into parts.

Commentary

The three-way conversation will encourage children to remember to start a new line for each speaker and, when splitting direct speech into parts, children will have to think carefully about where to include commas, inverted commas, full stops and capital letters.

The importance of this part of the lesson is that they are applying their new knowledge in a purposeful context and you are able to monitor and assess their understanding, addressing misconceptions as they arise.

Plenary

Explain to the children that you have written the ending of the story but have forgotten how to write direct speech. Hand out some pre-prepared sentences relating to the story with all punctuation missing. Make sure that you differentiate accordingly. Ask the children to work in pairs to 'correct' the sentences using a marker pen and collect these to include on your working wall.

Commentary

This activity will provide immediate feedback as to children's understanding of direct speech and the use of appropriate punctuation. If you ask children to do this in pairs, they will be able to discuss their choices and argue their case. You will be able to listen in on these conversations and gain further insight into how well they have understood the lesson. Your class will also be able to refer to these on the working wall, ensuring that they continue to use direct speech effectively across the curriculum.

Assessment (measuring achievement)

Assessment for learning

Do not assume that all children will begin this lesson with the same degree of understanding about the use of direct speech.

- Ask key questions to determine how much children know: Why have you put the speech marks there? Can you think of an alternative to 'said'? How do we know when the character is speaking? Where do I include the exclamation mark? What does this tell us about the character?

- Ask children to identify speech during shared or guided reading sessions. Encourage them to change their voice when characters are speaking. Are they aware that speech marks indicate that someone is speaking? Do they change their voice according to the adverb or verb used to describe how the character is speaking? Use a wide variety of books that include speech, for example, *Good Little Wolf* by Nadia Shireen, *Billy's Bucket* by Kes Gray and Garry Parsons, *The Gruffalo* by Julia Donaldson and Axel Scheffler and just about anything by Roald Dahl.

- Use drama sessions to ask children to verbalise their thoughts whilst in character and then write them down on sticky notes using the conventions of direct speech.

Assessment at the point of learning

You will need to assess learning throughout the lesson so that you are able to provide the correct amount of challenge for all learners.

- Take full advantage of mini-whiteboards to allow children to demonstrate what they know. They may be able to use inverted commas correctly, but have they remembered to include the full stop or question mark within the speech marks?

- Encourage other adults working within the classroom to make a note of children who are having difficulties and address this immediately with the child, exploring misconceptions and modelling correct use of speech punctuation.

- Ask children to explain why they have used specific verbs or adverbs to describe how a character is speaking. Do they understand why they need to include speech marks? Are they beginning a new line for a different speaker? How can you make this explicit in your teaching?

Assessment of learning

Have the children achieved the objective of the lesson and how do you know?

- During the plenary, are children still making the same mistakes or have they moved on during the course of the lesson?

- Are they enclosing the speaker's exact words within speech marks?

- Do they start each piece of speech with a capital letter?

- Have they used a comma in the correct place when direct speech comes after the name of the speaker?

- Have they started a new line for each speaker?

Furthermore, does the inclusion of dialogue in the text contribute to the overall effect of the writing? If children are simply including speech in order to fulfil a 'checklist' of criteria, they may not understand how it can fundamentally change a piece of writing and add to the tone, atmosphere and mood. When marking work, make comments explicit and refer directly to the learning objectives so that learners are aware of their success and how they can continue to move forward.

Challenges

Some children may have a limited understanding of punctuation and so this will need consolidating prior to teaching speech marks. Use punctuation fans and bingo games to provide opportunities for children to become familiar with different types of punctuation.

- Some children may benefit from a more visual approach and so try large speech bubble templates to write speech before adding it to text. Children who prefer an auditory approach may benefit from watching short film clips and identifying the speech within this context.

- The use of drama to reinforce conventions of written speech will often support pupils for whom English is as an additional language as it provides opportunities for pupils to be more aware of their language use and orally rehearse their thoughts before committing them to paper.

Application of learning

Links to other areas of the curriculum

Direct speech is usually associated with narrative as it contributes to the setting of the scene, moves the action of the scene forward, gives an insight into characterisation and informs the reader as to intent. The lesson above illustrates how direct speech can be used in fictional stories. However, direct speech may be included in reports and recounts where there is a need to report what someone has said. These may be explored through:

- History: writing a historical recount;

- PHSE: writing conversations that explore moral dilemmas;

- eye-witness reports: writing statements describing an event or a situation.

Next lesson

Convert a play script into narrative dialogue using the conventions of speech. Use this lesson to teach the children how to use dialogue sparingly and for effect. Break up the dialogue with description and use time connectives to signal the passing of time, demonstrating how speech can be powerful when used for a specific purpose. Explain to the children that, as the reader, we do not necessarily need to read every single word of a conversation to get a feel for how the plot may unravel. Demonstrate how to use their writing to hint at what might happen next rather than through the use of a character's spoken words. In this way, you will be teaching your class how to use speech effectively to enhance narrative rather than to detract from it.

Continue to remind children how to use direct speech effectively in subsequent lessons. Although your focus may have changed, children still need to apply this knowledge when working independently.

Learning outcomes review

Direct speech can be complex and there is a lot for children to remember. You should now feel more confident when approaching the teaching of direct speech and have a good understanding of the rules and conventions associated with dialogue. You will know why children need to learn about direct speech and understand some of the ways in which it can be used to define character and contribute to the setting of the scene. In addition, you should now have ideas for creating lessons that allow you to teach direct speech and be able to address some of the challenges that you may face when teaching children how to use direct speech effectively.

Points to consider

- How might you use shared writing to teach other aspects of grammar?
- How could you further scaffold learning so that all children are able to use direct speech in their writing?
- In what other ways might you use drama to teach specific grammatical devices?

Further reading

Crystal, D. (2008) *Making Sense of Grammar*. Harlow: Longman.

This book clearly outlines the conventions of speech punctuation.

Department for Education and Employment (DfEE) (2000) *Grammar for Writing*. London: DfEE.

This resource is no longer in print but is available online. Although produced in 2000, unit 4 for Year 3 includes some very useful activities to use when teaching direct speech.

Gamble, N. (2013) *Exploring Children's Literature: Reading with Pleasure and Purpose*, 3rd edn. London: Sage.

The chapter on 'Aspects of narrative: character setting and theme' contains descriptions of the different ways speech is represented in text.

www.bbc.co.uk/learningzone/clips/speech-marks/747.html

This short clip explores the use of speech punctuation and is ideal to use in the classroom to illustrate how to use direct speech.

References

Cherry, L. (2000) *The Great Kapok Tree.* Florida: Voyager Books.

Clarke, S. (2001) *Unlocking Formative Assessment.* London: Hodder and Stoughton.

Department for Education (DfE) (2013) *The National Curriculum in England: Framework Document.* London: DfE.

Donaldson, J. and Scheffler, A. (1999) *The Gruffalo.* London: Macmillan Children's Books.

Gray, K. and Parsons, G. (2004) *Billy's Bucket.* London: Random House Children's Publishers UK.

Ings, R. (2009) *Writing Is Primary: Action Research on the Teaching of Writing in Primary Schools.* London: Esme Fairbairn Foundation.

Ofsted (2009) *English at the Crossroads: An Evaluation of English in Primary and Secondary Schools.* London: Ofsted.

Shireen, N. (2011) *Good Little Wolf.* London: Random House Children's Publishers UK.

Chapter 6

Year 3: Using the perfect tense

Learning outcomes

The way verbs can change depending on time, cause and number is one of the most difficult concepts to explore with children, and relies on a significant amount of prior learning. This chapter investigates what children need to recognise in their own speech and wider reading in order to develop their knowledge of verbs and the perfect tense.

This chapter will allow you to achieve the following outcomes:

- understand what is meant by the perfect tense;
- develop an understanding of how the auxiliary verb *to have* can be used to express precise grammatical meaning.

Teachers' Standards

Working through this chapter will help you meet the following standards:

2. Promote good progress and outcomes by pupils.
3. Demonstrate good subject and curriculum knowledge.
4. Plan and teach well-structured lessons.

Links to the National Curriculum

Lower Key Stage 2 statutory requirement

Years 3 and 4

READING

Comprehension

Pupils should be taught to:

- understand what they read, in books they can read independently, by:

    ✓ identifying how language, structure, and presentation contribute to meaning

Vocabulary, grammar and punctuation

Pupils should be taught to:

- develop their understanding of the concepts set out in Appendix 2 by:

  ✓ using the present perfect form of verbs in contrast to the past tense

- use and understand the grammatical terminology in Appendix 2 accurately and appropriately when discussing their writing and reading.

(DfE, 2013)

Key focus: The perfect tense

The perfect tense refers to a particular grammatical structure which combines the auxiliary verb *have* with the past participle of a main verb within a clause. There are two forms: the present perfect and the past perfect. In order to understand the perfect tense as a verb aspect, children must look at how auxiliary verbs are used in the English language, in particular the three primary verbs (*be, have* and *do*). The Primary Curriculum for English from 2014 states that children should be taught *the present and past tenses correctly and consistently including the progressive form* in Year 2, the progressive form being the use of the verb *be* along with the -ing form of a main verb to express a continuous event (DfE, 2013). In Years 3 and 4 this is then developed to include the study of the perfect.

There is some disagreement between grammarians over the use of the label 'perfect tense' to describe the use of the verb *to have* when constructing verb phrases. David Crystal (1988) prefers to describe them as perfective and progressive verb aspects rather than tenses to distinguish them from the model provided by Latin, which has a series of verb endings to indicate meaning that can only be translated through the use of auxiliary verbs. For example, the verb *to learn* (*disco* in Latin) can be easily conjugated or modified from its basic form like this:

didicî	I have learned
didicistî	You (sg.) have learned
didicit	He/she/it has learned
didicimus	We have learned
didicistis	You (pl.) have learned
didicêrunt	They have learned

However in *The Penguin Dictionary of English Grammar*, R. L. Trask warns that *the perfective should not be confused with the PERFECT* (sic). *In spite of the unfortunate similarity of their names, the two are entirely distinct* (Trask, 2000). This inconsistency in terminology can make it difficult for teachers to unpick precisely how to introduce these concepts to children, so for the purposes of the lesson detailed here we shall use the term *perfect tense*, as this is how it is referred to in the National Curriculum from 2014 (DfE, 2013).

Think about the meaning of the following statements, made using *have* and a main verb, in this case *climb*, *run*, *crawl* and *scale*:

> I have climbed the highest mountains
> I have run through the fields
> I have run, I have crawled
> I have scaled these city walls

You may recognise these as song lyrics (*I still haven't found what I'm looking for*, by U2): they ably demonstrate the way the present perfect tense is used in order to indicate that the action continues to be true up to and including the present. Consider the effect of changing the verb aspect to the past perfect:

> I had climbed the highest mountains
> I had run through the fields
> I had run, I had crawled
> I had scaled these city walls

This places the action firmly in the past, events that do not have any current relevance. Now consider the way the meaning changes if we remove the verb *have* altogether:

> I climbed the highest mountains
> I ran through the fields
> I ran, I crawled
> I scaled these city walls

Activity

Try to articulate how the present perfect, past perfect and past tense examples above are different in their meaning. What is the effect on the reader of this relatively minor change in sentence structure?

How children learn about perfect tense

By Year 3 children will have been introduced to the idea that the verb helps us understand when an event happens (I *went* to the shop yesterday; you *go* to bed now) or the state of being of an object/subject (I think, therefore I am). They will be familiar with the way a verb changes when it is used to describe an event taking place in the past as opposed to the present, and know that some verbs are regular, i.e., follow predictable rules when changing from present to past tense, and that some are irregular and the past tense form needs to be learned. Children will understand that the verb *have* (along with *be* and *do*) can act as a main verb (I have a chocolate biscuit) and now you are introducing them to the idea that it can also be used as an auxiliary to help other verbs to create the present perfect and the past perfect tense. The word *auxiliary* is defined by the *Oxford English Dictionary* (**www. oed.com/**) as meaning *providing supplementary or additional help and support*, but what kind of support does the main verb need? Verbs indicate time by changing form from the infinitive (present tense, often preceded by the word 'to') to an alternative spelling which indicates the past, for example comb/combed; shop/shopped; keep/kept; use/used. The addition of the verb *have* in front of the past participle helps specify the time in which the event takes place.

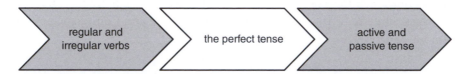

Figure 6.1   Learning about the perfect tense

Children need to understand that, though both the present perfect and the past perfect tense deal with things that have already happened (anterior time), the present perfect details the relevance of an earlier action to the present, while the past perfect details the relevance of an earlier action to the time in the past being discussed (or even an event that might have been but is in fact unreal, such as what might have been; such as if England had won the World Cup, or if Neil Armstrong hadn't landed on the moon). This can be achieved through identifying many examples and discussing the effect created by the writer: a collection of extracts from a range of fiction and non-fiction texts as a resource library for this would be highly beneficial for this sort of activity, so it is important you use your reading of a wide range of texts for children to gather source material.

Teaching your class: Year 3

The children in Year 3 will already know that verbs are instrumental to clause, and thus sentence, structure. What is important at this stage is the use of multi-sensory approaches which will help them make sense of abstract concepts such as time passing and current relevance. It would also be helpful to link this to a cross-curricular area, such as History, to give the children meaningful contexts to apply their learning.

Context

This Year 3 class are familiar with the use of drama and physical activities in their language learning. They have investigated the use of powerful verbs in their writing for dramatic effect, and have a clear understanding of the way verbs which denote actions work; they are beginning to secure their understanding of verbs that denote a state of being. Previous lessons have introduced the children to the infinitive form of verbs, and a range of laminated cards with examples have been prepared: to dance, to jump, to walk, etc.

Learning objectives

- To identify how the use of the perfect tense contributes to meaning by indicating the relevance of an event to the current time.

- To be able to create sentences using the perfect tense.

Commentary

The objectives for the lesson need to be small in number as this can be a very difficult abstract concept for children. The objectives above can be visible from the beginning of the lesson, but should not be unpicked until the main section: this will allow children time to reactivate prior learning without trying to predict or guess where the lesson is going and thus miss the chance to focus on the understanding needed to engage with the new learning.

Lesson opener: To infinitive and beyond!

Explain that you are going to be selecting volunteers to create a chain reaction of change by constructing a sentence word by word and that the class needs to listen carefully. During the activity, when they hear something wrong they need to call 'Freeze' and the children at the front modelling the activity must stand still. Select a pupil to be the 'infinitive verb' by giving him or her a card with a verb written on it. Ask the pupil to read the card, for example *to dance*, and ask the child to repeat it over and over while acting the verb ('To dance, to dance, to dance, to dance . . .'). Select another pupil to be the 'pronoun' *I*; again ask that pupil to repeat the pronoun over and over ('I, I, I, I, I, I, I, I, I . . .') while holding the card visible to the class. Ask the pronoun to join the verb in whatever activity they are taking part in, and they should connect by linking arms/joining hands. At this stage encourage them to alternate between their words (I/to dance/I/to dance) to show they are now linked. A member of the class should call 'Freeze': ask them if the new chain sounds right, and if not, explain what is wrong, allowing them to seek help from other members of the class if they find it difficult to articulate the reason. They should identify that the word 'to' has become superfluous and should be left out. Restart the verb/pronoun chant, which should now be 'I/dance, I/dance . . .' Hand out a final card with a time adverbial (*yesterday*): the teacher should then place this child between the others and relink them.

Again they should repeat their words in order (remembering to demonstrate the verb!). After they have repeated 'I/yesterday/dance, I/yesterday/dance', the class should recognise this is incorrect and call 'Freeze', explaining that the adverbial is in the wrong place. Further discussion should identify that the verb needs to change again to reflect that the action is now described as having happened in the past, although you may have to restart the chant before this is realised.

> ## Commentary
>
> This is an activity based on the teaching ideas of a foreign languages teacher working in a primary environment. By starting with kinaesthetic or tactile approaches you are reminding the children of the principles of verb/tense agreement in an engaging way, and removing the idea that grammar is boring and desk-based. Learning about language and linguistics should be exciting; this is, after all, the way we communicate within our social world, and should be presented as an opportunity rather than a chore. Make sure you keep the activity fast-paced and active, treating it as a competitive game against the clock.

Give out a selection of infinitive verbs, pronouns and words indicating time to the children to work on in pairs and ask them to construct sentences on whiteboards using the different pronouns and time adverbials (see Chapter 7 for more on adverbials). Encourage them to 'act out' their verbs where appropriate to help them understand what they are writing. After five minutes, get them to explain to another pair how the verb looks in each of their sentences and why. Did they need to add any other words to their sentences to create meaning, for example, *will* when describing an event that will happen in the future?

> ## Commentary
>
> Although this is a collaborative exercise this activity will allow you to address any misconceptions prior to introducing the idea of the perfect tense.
>
> Examples of time adverbials that could be shared with the children on printed cards may include words such as 'previously', 'last week', 'formerly', 'yesterday'. Avoid future time, such as 'next week' or 'tomorrow', as this would require the use of modal verbs such as 'will' and 'shall' (explored in more depth in Chapter 9). However, children who might benefit from being challenged can be set the task of developing their own future tense sentences, the explanation of which can then be used as the start of the main activity.
>
> For the verbs, encourage children to reflect on the difference between regular verbs, such as 'skate', 'walk', 'achieve', and irregular verbs, such as 'eat', 'run', 'drive', as part of the discussion.

Main lesson

Introduction

Show children the Guided Group Sign-up Sheet (Table 6.1): this should have a breakdown of some of the steps that lead towards the main objectives in the form of questions.

Table 6.1   Guided group sign-up sheet

Guided topic	Names
What does 'auxiliary' mean?	
What is an auxiliary verb?	
What do we mean by past tense?	

Explain that as the lesson progresses the children can sign up for guided support from the teacher, which will be done during independent learning activities in the following English lesson. The spaces on the sheet are for children to pose their own questions as they arise, so they can identify the gaps in their own knowledge and provide the focus for the guided sessions.

Commentary

The Teachers' Standards require teachers to promote good progress and outcomes by pupils and one of the suggested ways you can demonstrate this is by encouraging pupils to take a responsible and conscientious attitude to their own work and study. By providing the children with the opportunity to select what aspects they would like your guidance on you are enabling them to be responsible for their own learning, thus demonstrating your own ability to meet this standard. Of course, the success of this strategy is entirely dependent on your knowledge of the grammatical terms and rules being learned, so it is vital you also demonstrate good subject and curriculum knowledge through addressing your own misunderstandings (DfE, 2012, p7): the further reading suggested throughout this book will help with this!

Remind children of the progressive aspect, where the main verb is preceded by the verb *to be*, for example:

> The children are singing.
> The dog is jumping.
> The ship was sinking.

(N.B.: If any children worked on sentences involving modal verbs to write about events set in the future, this can be discussed instead of the progressive aspect.)

Using individual whiteboards, get the children to identify the number of verbs in each sentence. They should recognise that there are two in each of the examples above. Ask them to identify which words they think are the main verbs.

Commentary

The progressive, which the National Curriculum for England (2014) introduces in Year 2 (DfE, 2013), is more prevalent in speech and can be used to discuss and analyse the difference between writing and speaking to an audience; it can also be used to detail specific events, habits and states of being.

It is through such discussions that the children will begin to understand how each structure can be used in their own writing, even if they feel hesitant in giving their own definitions. Reminding the children of the progressive tenses will prepare them for the concept of the perfect tense as a combination of auxiliary and main verb.

Introduce the term *auxiliary verb*. Using an image of an auxiliary nurse (a Clip Art or stock image will be fine; even better would be a teacher-in-role if you feel confident enough!), ask children to try and work out what an *auxiliary* is. They should begin to come up with suggestions such as an auxiliary fixes or helps. Explain that there are three primary auxiliary verbs: they have already looked at one of them *(be)* and now they are going to look at how the word *have* can act as an auxiliary to help other verbs.

Use the cards from earlier (pronoun/verb/adverbial) or prepare a resource for the interactive whiteboard. Attach a selection, including regular and irregular verbs, to the board, this time adding the verb *have*. Using talk partners, give the children one minute to come up with a sentence which includes *have* next to one of the main verbs. Select pairs to say their sentences: using thumbs up/thumbs down, ask the class to indicate if they think the sentence sounds right or wrong. If thumbs go down, allow the pair to select a member of the class to explain what they think was wrong. By allowing them to select who will critique their answer you are encouraging the children to feel safe and confident about this sort of peer review.

Commentary

It is important at this stage that the children are able to distinguish between the different forms of regular and irregular verbs. For example, if the verb is 'eat' they will have changed it to 'ate' during the starter activity, but when you combine it with 'have' to create the present perfect tense it becomes 'eaten'.

Tell the children they have just created the present perfect tense (with drum roll for dramatic effect!). Explain this is a grammatical feature, but that you need them to work out what it does for the reader. Put talk partners into mixed-ability groups of four and give them an A3 piece of paper with three examples of the present perfect tense, and give them up to ten minutes to be 'linguistic detectives', analysing the evidence in front of them to develop their theory to explain what the present perfect tense does. An extension task is to have two examples of the past perfect for groups who finish quickly, enabling them to think about the difference in effect.

Examples of present perfect sentences can come from a range of children's books but ultimately can be kept quite simple, for example:

- I have written a letter to Father Christmas to ask for a skateboard.

- Sophie has walked all the way home in the rain.

- She has dried her coat on the radiator.

- Jamal has finished his dinner and now wants dessert.

- He has played football since he was little.

- You have given me your cold and now I can't stop sneezing.

- The pupils have discussed the sentences in groups.

- They have worked hard during this lesson.

During this task you may have children signing up for the guided groups. Encourage them to pose their own questions, but avoid starting the 'mini-lessons' during this time as the children will miss valuable discussion time with their peers. Instead, ensure you build time into the next English lesson by organising a series of independent practical application tasks.

Commentary

Personalising learning or differentiation does not mean more work: it means offering more challenge. However, in this case, as the groups should be mixed-ability, it is worth having the extension task for any group that needs it. If you do decide to ability group your class you might wish to offer different selections of sentences; at this point you will need to think about who is most likely to need to be guided through the 'investigation' to ensure quality discussion. For further information on quality discussion see details of the Thinking Together project at **http://thinkingtogether. educ.cam.ac.uk/resources/5_examples_of_talk_in_groups.pdf.**

Attach the annotated sheets to the walls around the classroom and get the children to look at other groups' annotations. Did each group reach the same conclusion? Who do they think gave the best explanation of the effect of the present tense in someone's writing?

Practical application

Following this lesson, children should be given opportunities to write in this way, for example:

- Ask them to write sentences for a 'Things I have achieved' display.

- Write stories that include dialogue and set a class target of including perfect tense phrases in the speech.

- Set the children the challenge of finding out what hobbies their classmates do outside school, and who has done it the longest. Use this to create graphs, and use present tense phrases as labels, e.g. 'Has been going to Cubs', 'Has played the recorder'.

Commentary

Think about when the perfect tense is used most frequently and build in opportunities for purposeful application in order to capitalise on their developing understanding. The more frequently they link this sort of investigation to their own work as writers, the more it will have a purpose. But beware of making arbitrary links: try not to shoehorn the perfect tense where it does not belong!

Plenary

Take an extract from a children's novel and ask the children to identify examples of the perfect and progressive tense. Encourage them to annotate the text and then discuss the effect of both. The extracts below contain examples of the present and past perfect, which would allow you to see who can make the link between the present and past tense of the verb *have*, although the present perfect is represented by the contraction -*'ve*, so is not immediately obvious. Both extracts are from *The Great Ghost Rescue* by Eva Ibbotson and demonstrate how the extract does not have to be long to enable children to show what they know.

> 'Is everything alright?'
>
> 'Mm. We've got to London. But I've kind of collected rather a lot more than I started with.'
>
> And he told her about Walter the Wet, and the Mad Monk, and the vampire bats.
>
> 'Goodness! It's like the Pied Piper of Hamelin,' said Barbara. 'You'll need an absolutely *enormous* sanctuary.'
>
> And then she told him what she had found out since Rick had gone.
>
> The Mad Monk was as happy as the rest of them. He had found a small, ruined chapel – nothing more than four walls open to the sky with a mound of stones where the altar had been

but it suited him beautifully. 'Oh, the quiet, oh the peace,' he mumbled. 'I shall be able to pull myself together here. Look at my ectoplasm! It's looking healthier already, don't you think?' And he wandered off to show his muscles (which certainly looked less like cold porridge than they had done) to Aunt Hortensia.

Commentary

By text-marking an extract and discussing the writer's use of the perfect and the progressive tense the children are seeing these verb aspects modelled by 'experts'; it also enables you to see whether they can recognise these elements of sentence structure. Like the present perfect, the progressive aspect is difficult to recognise initially as it is in the form of a contraction: 'It's looking'. The three examples of the past perfect ('There he had found '; 'the altar had been'; 'they had done') are all linked to irregular verbs and thus can't be identified by the -ed ending.

Assessment (measuring achievement)

Assessment for learning

- The activity at the start of the lesson will enable you to clear up any confusion or misunderstanding about past tense and verb forms. Monitor the discussions during the paired work in order to ensure all children have a consolidated understanding of the concept of past tense.

- The guided work sign-up sheet will enable pupils to identify gaps in their own understanding and self-assess their needs. Ensure you pick this up, grouping concepts where appropriate, and build this in to your teaching as soon as possible. A delay will mean that the children will lose the impetus and the teaching will lack coherence.

Assessment at the point of learning

- The discussions and annotations will enable you to assess the children's understanding. Use open questions to prompt groups that get stuck, and if any group is modelling effective talk, praise them for the specific way they are working well together without halting the discussion for long.

Assessment of learning

This needs to be explicitly linked back to the lesson's learning objectives. Have the children achieved the following?

- To identify how the use of the perfect tense contributes to meaning by indicating the relevance of an event to the current time.

- To be able to create sentences using the perfect tense.

Much of the assessment of learning for individuals will come from the discussions and work on the whiteboard, so think carefully about how you will record your observations, e.g. sticky notes, mark book record of the learning objective, children's self-assessments.

Challenges

- Children will need to have a secure knowledge of verb forms: some children may struggle with the various forms of irregular verbs, for example. This may need a lot of support during the lesson to enable them to engage with the learning.

- There may be some confusion over the use of the verb *have* as an auxiliary and as a main. You may need to unpick this, especially if children identify every instance of the word have/has/had as being an example of the perfect tense.

Application of learning

Links to other areas of the curriculum

The perfect tense is largely unique to English within the UK, and is used to make the link between the present and the past when describing an action. This may appear across the curriculum through:

- Science: recording observations, for example 'the flower has grown significantly since it was measured last week';

- History: past perfect can be used to explore alternatives to real-life events, for example, what might have happened if the Romans had not invaded Britain? What wouldn't we have had (aqueducts, viaducts, Monty Python sketches about aqueducts and viaducts . . .)?

- English: precision in narrative writing.

Next lesson

Think about the way some verbs have multiple forms to indicate past tense, for example:

> I ate the cake/I have eaten the cake
>
> You broke the vase/you have broken the vase
>
> She drove the car to work/she has driven the car to work

How can these irregular simple past and past participle verb forms be explored with the children? Also, consider the way that auxiliary verbs allow for negation and inversion. We don't say, 'Harry runs not' or 'Beth sleepn't'; we also stay away from sentence structures such as, 'Walked you here?' or 'Flew you on a plane?'

Learning outcomes review

You should now understand what is meant by the perfect tense and understand how it can link the present to the past. You should also be confident in teaching the children about auxiliary verbs and how they can help a main verb to demonstrate the specific time an event happened. The lesson plan and commentary demonstrate how the children can be included in the assessment of their own progression, and you should feel confident in encouraging them to be active participants in the process.

Points to consider

- How might you use other investigations to consolidate this aspect of grammar?
- In what ways could you use physical activities prior to writing as a warm-up for thinking about sentence structure?
- The verb *to do* is also a primary verb (although sometimes referred to as a dummy verb), i.e., can be used as a main verb and an auxiliary. How might you introduce this to children's learning? And when do you think it is appropriate?

Further reading

Crystal, D. (1996) *Discover Grammar*. Harlow: Longman.

This book provides some explanation of what Crystal terms the perfective and progressive verb aspects along with helpful activities to help consolidate your understanding.

Mercer, N. (2000) *Words and Minds: How We Use Language to Think Together*. London: Routledge.

This book preceded the Thinking Together project mentioned in this chapter and provides explanations of the different ways talk can be used effectively in the classroom as well as excellent insights into why talk doesn't always work to move thinking forward.

References

Crystal, D. (1988) *Rediscover Grammar*. Harlow: Longman.

Department for Education (DfE) (2012) *Teachers' Standards*. London: DfE.

Department for Education (DfE) (2013) *The National Curriculum in England: Framework Document*. London: DfE.

Ibbotson, E. (1975) *The Great Ghost Rescue*. London: Macmillan.

Trask, R. L. (2000) *The Penguin Dictionary of English Grammar*. London: Penguin.

Chapter 7

Year 4: Teaching adverbial phrases

Learning outcomes

This chapter looks at how to teach adverbial phrases. It explores what children need to learn, what you need to know in order to teach them and how children learn.

This chapter will allow you to achieve the following outcomes:

- increase awareness of different types of adverbials;
- develop understanding of the use of adverbials and how they enhance writing;
- develop understanding of how to teach adverbial phrases.

Teachers' Standards

Working through this chapter will help you meet the following standards:

3. Demonstrate good subject and curriculum knowledge.
4. Plan and teach well-structured lessons.
5. Adapt teaching to respond to the strengths and needs of all pupils.
6. Make accurate and productive use of assessment.

Links to the National Curriculum

Lower Key Stage 2 statutory requirement

Years 3 and 4
Pupils should be taught to:

- develop their understanding of the concepts set out in Appendix 2 by:

  ✓ extending the range of sentences with more than one clause by using a wider range of conjunctions, e.g. when, if, because, although
  ✓ using conjunctions, adverbs and prepositions to express time and cause
  ✓ using fronted adverbials
  ✓ learning the grammar for years 3 and 4 in English Appendix 2

- indicate grammatical and other features by:

  ✓ using commas after fronted adverbials

- use and understand the grammatical terminology in Appendix 2 accurately and appropriately when discussing their writing and reading.

(DfE, 2013)

Key focus: The use of adverbials

In order to be effective writers, children need to understand how adverbial phrases can change the meaning and add precision to any text type. The inclusion of an adverbial phrase in their writing will demonstrate children's ability to use adventurous vocabulary and will engage the reader by clarifying meaning beyond simple description.

To teach children about the use of adverbials, you need to understand the function of an adverb within a sentence. The not-so-humble adverb is often hugely misrepresented within primary grammar teaching. Far from being a mere '-ly' word, the adverb is used to do a range of jobs, from placing the action in a space or time to making adjectives seem less or more than they are. An *adverbial phrase* is a group of words that can modify a verb, an adjective or another verb.

Adverbs in their simplest form are used to provide further information about the verb in the sentence and relate to time (when?), place (where?) and process (how?). They are used to describe a verb and can comprehensively build up a picture of the character, setting or atmosphere by adding extra information. They are used within sentences to add precise meaning to an action, for example, 'the cat entered the room' becomes '*silently*, the cat entered the room'. The adverb modifies the verb by describing how the cat moves and suggests that there is a reason as to why the cat's entrance is silent.

Adverbs that describe how something happens are known as process adverbials and can refer to the *manner* in which something is carried out, the *means* by which something is achieved, the *instrument* through which an action is completed and the *agent* through which something happens.

- I ate my ice cream *quickly*. (manner)

- She travelled *by bus*. (means)

- I ate my ice cream *with a large spoon*. (instrument)

- I was hit *by a football*. (agent)

Spatial adverbs can refer to *distance*, *direction* or *position* and are used to add extra information to a sentence in order to clarify meaning. Spatial adverbs describe where the action of a verb is carried out, thus allowing the writer to describe a setting.

- The mountains loomed ominously *in the distance*. (distance)

- It appeared *from out of nowhere*. (direction)

- They occupied *the first floor*. (position)

Temporal adverbs are concerned with time and will contribute to the atmosphere of a piece of writing. They will also help to move events forward and are used to denote a specified time, frequency or duration.

- The parcel arrived *this morning*. (specified time)

- The clock chimed *every hour*. (frequency)

- The music lasted *for two minutes*. (duration)

Children need to be able to recognise adverbials in their reading and have opportunities to discuss the writer's use of these in order to convey precise meaning. Do they know what they are looking for? Why does the author use a particular word or phrase to describe how, why or when something happens in the story? In essence, children need to read 'good' writing so that they are able to gain an understanding of the linguistic requirements of texts and explore how writers manipulate sentences to achieve the required effect. In order to move children on effectively in their learning it is essential that we develop this through modelling the construction of adverbials within a range of text types.

Activity

Look at the following adverbials and categorise them according to whether they are process, spatial or temporal adverbs. Can you put them into a sentence?

fiercely	regularly	in the distance
this morning	outside	furiously
straight away	smoothly	every hour
yesterday	eventually	foolishly

You may have chosen the word *furiously* as a process adverbial and constructed a sentence such as:

> Furiously, she slammed the door hard.

What you have done is modified the verb (*slammed*), adding detail to the sentence so as to clarify meaning and provide a context for the action that takes place. This provides the reader with a clear picture of events and communicates meaning effectively and precisely.

How children learn about adverbials

Adverbial is an umbrella term for a word or group of words that form part of a clause. They provide extra information or links between sentences. Children should already be familiar with using adverbs to modify the verb from work they have been doing in Key Stage 1 and Year 3. They are more than likely able to use words such as *quietly*, *cautiously* and *silently* to add meaning to their sentences and will probably be able to list many more *-ly* words. The next stage is to use adverbial phrases which are specifically groups of words that modify the verb and these are the focus for the following lesson. Finally, adverbial clauses such as those identified in the following sentences should be the next step.

> We started the game *as soon as our friends turned up.*

> *After we had eaten*, we went for a long walk.

These are dependent clauses that modify verbs and verb phrases. The dependent clause cannot stand alone and requires another independent clause to create a sentence that is grammatically correct. It is important that dependent clauses are explored in more detail as part of the learning continuum once children are secure in their use of adverbs and adverbial phrases.

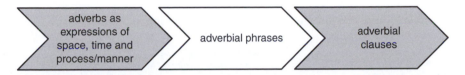

Figure 7.1 Learning about adverbials

Although the terminology may be unfamiliar to the children, it is likely that they will have an understanding of how adverbials can change the meaning of a sentence. As children become more confident in their choice of adverbials, they will begin to experiment with language and try out new words. It is important that you explore these choices with children so that they select adverbs and adverbial phrases that convey appropriate meaning. Point them out during guided reading and ask children to explain what effect they have upon the sentence. You can encourage children to highlight adverbials in their written work and try changing them. What does this do to the meaning of the sentence? Use the correct terms with the children so that they feel confident when discussing their work with yourself and others.

Teaching your class

The lesson outlined below is intended as a starting point for teaching a lesson on adverbials with Year 4 children and will provide opportunities to explore how you can teach elements of grammar with the purpose of enhancing children's written work. Far from teaching adverbials in isolation as a grammar exercise, children need to have a clearly defined purpose and context for using adverbials to improve their work. Consider how you would address the differing needs of the children.

Context

The pupils in Year 4 have been exploring adventure and mystery stories. To ensure pupils have a purpose and a 'real' context for their writing, you could write a letter in role as an author asking for some ideas for new stories, set up a class story-writing competition or ask the local library to write to the class asking for some stories to display. In all of these cases, the emphasis should be on wanting pupils to write stories that convey a mysterious atmosphere through use of descriptive vocabulary. The pupils in this Year 4 class have already visited the forest area in school, the park and a local castle as part of their unit of work for this term and have spent some time identifying and using adjectives and powerful verbs in their writing so as to excite and interest the reader. They are now extending this work to incorporate the use of adverbial phrases in their writing.

Learning objectives

- To be able to identify adverbial phrases.

- To be able to explain the effect of these sentences.

- To be able to apply adverbial phrases in our own writing.

Commentary

It is important that learning objectives are clear and concise and address the learning that you intend to take place. The verbs 'identify', 'explain' and 'apply' refer to specific skills that children will be practising and indicate that these are skills that can be applied in a variety of contexts. Subject knowledge is clearly identified within the learning objectives in terms of the grammatical feature that children will be learning about and applying in their own work. You will be able to assess the learning against the learning objectives by identifying children who are able to highlight various adverbials, listening to children talk about their use of adverbials and when marking their written work either as part of a guided writing session or through looking at their independent work.

Table 7.1 Planning work with adverbials

Lesson sequence	Grouping and organisation	Suggested resources
Starter	Children need to be sitting as a class and in mixed-ability groups	<ul><li>Tablets (iPads)</li><li>Mini-whiteboards</li><li>Writing journal</li><li>Sticky notes</li><li>Literacy books</li></ul>
Main lesson	Children are in groups according to ability	<ul><li>*Into the Forest* by Anthony Browne</li><li>*The Tunnel* by Anthony Browne</li><li>*Room on the Broom* by Julia Donaldson</li><li>*Where the Wild Things Are* by Maurice Sendak</li><li>**http://storybird.com/create/** is a useful website for pictures that provoke thought and lend themselves to descriptive writing</li></ul>
Plenary	Children at their tables	<ul><li>Sticky notes</li><li>Children's work</li><li>Highlighters</li></ul>

Starter: Where? When? How?

Show the class a number of sentences on laminated card or the whiteboard and ask them to identify when, where and how.

Pupils can use tablets, mini-whiteboards, writing journals and sticky notes or their Literacy books to record their answers so that you can begin to assess understanding.

Explain the terms *adverbials* and *adverbial phrases* as outlined above and define the three types of adverbials that are to be addressed during the course of this lesson and how they modify the verb.

For example:

Slowly, Tom appeared from out of the shadows.

Immediately she could see the car in the distance.

Commentary

This will help to address the misconception that adverbs are simply -ly words and will ensure that children focus on the when (immediately), where (out of the shadows; in the distance) and how (slowly) of the sentence. In doing so, they will be able to make connections between the information within the sentence and how it contributes to the meaning of the sentence as a whole. Use the correct terminology with the children: not only do they love 'technical' words, it allows you to develop that metalanguage within the classroom. It will provide you with an assessment for learning opportunity so that you are able to identify those children who are struggling to identify the different aspects of the sentence. You might then target these children within a guided group to address this.

Main lesson

Introduction

Show the class a picture as a stimulus to promote engagement, for example, an illustration from Anthony Browne's picture book *Into the Forest* or you could try using pictures from the suggestions in the suggested resources in Table 7.1 or finding pictures that relate to your class topic. Explain to the children that we are going to write sentences to describe what is happening in the book, using adverbial phrases and adverbs to indicate the precise meaning of the text.

In three groups the children discuss one of the following questions, linked explicitly to the starter activity:

When do you think this takes place? Partner talk and write suggestions on a mini-whiteboard. For example:

Early one morning . . .

This is the most challenging of the three tasks to complete because there are no explicit clues within the picture. This requires a high level of inference in order to make reasoned suggestions.

How do you think the boy is walking into the forest? Partner talk and write suggestions on a mini-whiteboard. For example, fearlessly . . .

This may be an easier task for the majority of pupils to complete because there will be more explicit clues within the picture, for example, facial expressions and body language.

Where do you think the scene is taking place? Partner talk and write suggestions on a mini-whiteboard. For example:

At the entrance to the forest . . .

This is potentially the easiest of the three tasks to complete because there will be more explicit clues within the picture which will indicate where the action is set.

Choose effective adverbials from the pupils' discussion in each of the categories and model writing the sentence, beginning a sentence with the chosen adverbial. For example:

Fearlessly, the boy entered the forest.

Early one morning, the boy set off on his journey.

At the entrance to the forest, the boy paused.

Reflect on how the adverbial phrase enhances the sentence and adds to the meaning of the text.

Critical questions to ask pupils:

- What does the adverbial phrase tell us as readers about the verb in each sentence?

- How does this help us understand more about what is happening?

- Why do you think the writer (the pupil) has chosen this particular word or phrase? Can the writer identify this for us by explaining his or her choice?

At this point it is vital that you model the process involved in selecting appropriate words and phrases through co-verbalisation of choices. The sentences have been selected from the children's writing and it is your role to ensure all are aware of why the choices were made and how the adverbial has contributed to the overall effect of the sentence.

Practical application

Children write the opening paragraph to their adventure story using adverbials to enhance their sentences. You will need to consider the use of prompts such as your working wall, scaffolded writing frames, vocabulary lists and microphones to record ideas to ensure that all children are able to achieve the learning objective.

Children need to use their knowledge of how adverbial phrases work to add detail to their writing. When writing the first paragraph of their story they can use space, time and process adverbials to set the scene. They are applying their knowledge straight away and it is much more meaningful to use them within the context of the opening paragraph to a story as it gives children a purpose for including them.

Plenary

Encourage pupils to swap with writing partners and identify the How? When? Where? information in the text. Ask pupils to give feedback to partners on how this adverbial phrase affected their understanding of the verb in the sentence. The writer explains the intended effect.

Through the use of peer assessment, ask pupils to identify how, why and when adverbial phrases and colour code these according to the type of adverbial used. Can they share with a partner how this adds to the atmosphere of their story? This enables pupils to reflect on their own learning and respond to feedback. During this part of the lesson it is important that you record any misconceptions relating to the lesson objectives in order to address them in subsequent teaching, including guided writing groups.

Assessment (measuring achievement)

Assessment for learning

It is important to assess prior learning before embarking upon this lesson.

- A starter activity at the beginning of the lesson may be employed so as to assess prior level of understanding with regard to adverbials.

- Identify adverbials in a shared text on the interactive whiteboard or ask pupils to highlight particular adverbials during guided reading sessions. This also provides pupils with opportunities to discuss meaning and purpose whilst supporting acquisition of a grammatical metalanguage. Which adverbials demand their attention? Do they have awareness that there are different types of adverbials? Why do they think the author has included a particular adverbial phrase?

- Record particularly effective adverbials that they have noted from their own reading in their journals to use in their own compositions.

Assessment at the point of learning

During the lesson, there are a number of opportunities to assess the pupils' learning and ensure that suitable challenges are set for all learners.

- The use of mini-whiteboards allows you, the teacher, to assess understanding of the different types of adverbials and address misconceptions at the point of learning.

- Ask the teaching assistant to make a note of pupils who have formulated effective adverbial phrases so that these can be extended during guided writing sessions.

- Similarly, the teaching assistant could identify those finding the task difficult, which would allow you to probe a little deeper.

Do they find it difficult to articulate meaning? Do they have the necessary vocabulary to use in this context? Have they an adequate understanding of the various types of adverbials? Are difficulties with transcriptional skills preventing pupils from writing effective sentences? All of these questions need to be answered if effective learning is to take place for all children.

Assessment of learning

You may want to ask yourself three key questions:

1. Have the pupils achieved the learning objectives?

2. How can we measure this?

3. What does this mean for the subsequent lesson?

Use key questions to elicit this information:

- How does the adverbial phrase make you feel?

- How does the character feel?

- How do we know?

- Would the setting have the same effect if an alternative adverbial phrase, describing when the action takes place, was used?

Use the plenary to make a summative assessment and follow this up when marking their written work or listening to their recordings of the story. Comment specifically on whether they have used adverbials and how this has created a specific effect on their writing.

Challenges

Limited vocabulary

Some pupils do not have the necessary vocabulary to describe certain situations and events. If you as the teacher do not supply these tools, pupils will be unable to get the job done. Use working walls, table prompts and lots of talk to build vocabulary. It might also be useful to carry out some 'shades of meaning' activities whereby pupils sort adverbs on a continuum, e.g. happily, cheerfully, gleefully, glumly, sadly, desperately for process adverbials. Pupils can sort spatial adverbial phrases in similar contexts, e.g. in the distance, far away, across the fields as opposed to nearby, beneath their feet.

- Pupils for whom English is an additional language (EAL). Visual prompts can be useful in supporting EAL pupils as they often require opportunities to draw on additional contextual support in order to understand new language that is being introduced. Pictures, moving images and drama activities can all enhance comprehension and can be used to good effect in this lesson plan to address further the needs of all learners.

- Pupils who may be reluctant to write. For some pupils, transcription may cause difficulties; they are unsure of spellings and sentence construction or do not have adequate fine motor control to sustain the physical act of writing over a period of time. In this case, recording stories, acting out scenarios and writing frames can all help encourage pupils to formulate their ideas and identify adverbial phrases in different contexts.

Application of learning

Links to other areas of the curriculum

Adverbials are about precision so are best suited to activities that require clear description. Although the examples used in the lesson are more easily applied to narrative there is potential for application in curriculum areas requiring explanations or recount. For example:

- Science: writing up observations during experiments;

- PSHE: describing feelings, actions and events;

- RE: sequencing events;

- History: describing and sequencing events.

Next steps

Although adverbials may not be the focus of the next lesson, it is important that you encourage children to continue using them in their writing. When completing the rest of their adventure and mystery story, ask children to identify where they have used adverbials and why. If some children are experiencing difficulties using appropriate adverbials you could ensure these children are brought together as a guided writing group and that you specifically address the use of adverbials by looking at paragraphs of their writing and encouraging children to explore their own writing with talk partners. Can they improve their work by identifying where they could use precise adverbials to indicate time, place and manner? Try scanning a paragraph from their writing and inserting adverbial phrases that do not make sense. Can they change them to adverbials that would enhance the text?

Learning outcomes review

The three learning outcomes for this chapter are all to do with adverbials and how you approach the teaching of adverbials with regard to developing your own subject knowledge and that of the children. You need to remember that adverbial phrases are used to add extra information to a sentence through defining *how, why* and *where*. Children can learn to include adverbials in a piece of writing and should be able to recognise them. However, what is important is that they use them to good effect and that the addition of these phrases enhances the writing. In this chapter we have explored how you can approach the teaching of adverbial phrases, and what you need to know in order to teach them effectively within the context of a Literacy lesson. We have presented an exemplar lesson plan, outlined the thinking behind the lesson and highlighted areas for assessment. You should be able to use the lesson plan for your own Year 3 class but it is more likely that you will use your professional judgement to adapt the plan to suit the needs of your particular class and the children you are teaching.

Points to consider

- In what other ways can pupils be encouraged to recognise the effect of specific word choices when describing events?
- How can you support the different learners in your class to achieve the learning objectives through the use of differentiated activities?
- How might you use the lesson idea to teach other aspects of grammar?

Further reading

Cremin, T. (2009) *Teaching English Creatively*. London: Routledge.

The chapter entitled 'Developing writers creatively – the later years' contains a section on teaching grammar and punctuation in context and deals with how you can apply this in descriptive writing.

Crystal, D. (1996) *Discover Grammar*. Essex: Pearson Education.

This is a useful book for exploring terminology and grammatical concepts and provides helpful exercises to secure subject knowledge.

References

Browne, A. (1992) *The Tunnel*. London: Walker Books.

Browne, A. (2004) *Into the Forest*. London: Walker Books.

Department for Education (DfE) (2013) *The National Curriculum in England: Framework Document*. London: DfE.

Donaldson, J. (2001) *Room on the Broom.* London: Macmillan Children's Books.

Sendak, M. (2000) *Where the Wild Things Are.* London: Random House Children's Publishers UK (first published 1963).

Chapter 8

Year 4: Teaching the difference between the plural and possessive -s

Learning outcomes

This chapter deals with a concept that crosses the boundary between grammar, punctuation and spelling: the use of the possessive apostrophe with plural nouns. On the face of it, this is not an issue of grammar at all; however children who do not grasp the grammatical difference between the different uses of -s as a suffix will find it difficult to make their meaning clear when writing.

This chapter will allow you to achieve the following outcomes:

- understand the grammatical differences between the plural and the possessive -s;
- understand how the correct use of the apostrophe can impact upon the meaning of individual words.

Teachers' Standards

Working through this chapter will help you meet the following standards:

3. Demonstrate good subject and curriculum knowledge.
4. Plan and teach well-structured lessons.
6. Make accurate and productive use of assessment.

Links to the National Curriculum

Lower Key Stage 2 statutory requirement

Years 3 and 4

WRITING

Transcription

Spelling (see English Appendix 1)

- Pupils should be taught to:

  ✓ place the possessive apostrophe accurately in words with regular plurals (for example, girls', boys') and in words with irregular plurals (for example, children's)

Vocabulary, grammar and punctuation

Pupils should be taught to:

- indicate grammatical and other features by:

  ✓ indicating possession by using the possessive apostrophe with plural nouns

- use and understand the grammatical terminology in Appendix 2 accurately and appropriately when discussing their writing and reading.

Appendix 2 – Year 4: Detail of content to be introduced (statutory requirement)

The grammatical difference between plural and possessive -s

(DfE, 2013)

Key focus: The many meanings of -s

In order to understand how the simple addition of an -s to the end of the word can have grammatical impact, it is important that you teach children to recognise it as a morpheme. The purpose behind this is summed up in the English National Curriculum for 2014, which states:

> *Pupils should be able to write down their ideas with a reasonable degree of accuracy and with good sentence punctuation. Teachers should therefore be consolidating pupils' writing skills, their vocabulary, their grasp of sentence structure and their knowledge of linguistic terminology.*

(DfE, 2013, p33)

Morphemes are units of meaning: by understanding the way letters and punctuation can be combined to change a word's meaning, children will be able to make appropriate spelling and vocabulary choices.

Morphemes can be free (unbound) or bound. Free morphemes are those that can stand alone as words, for example the letter pattern *ship* can be used on its own as a word, but it can also be used as a root word (*ship*ment), prefix (*ship*mate) or suffix (lady*ship*; premier*ship*). An -s added to the end of a word is a bound morpheme which changes the meaning of the word as a whole; in the case of a noun, it indicates an increase in number (Figure 8.1).

Even without the pictures you would know when one of something was being spoken about as opposed to a group of items because of the use of the -s. This minor change in spelling changes a noun from the singular to the plural.

Figure 8.1   From singular to plural

The addition of an apostrophe, however, changes the meaning again. Think about the difference between the following:

- Dogs/dog's

- Books/book's

- Pears/pear's

Although the words sound the same when spoken or read aloud, the use of the apostrophe changes the way we understand the meaning: *dog's* indicates to us that the following word will be something belonging to the dog. This combination of an apostrophe and -s is sometimes referred to as the genitive case.

Activity

- Write three short sentences – one for each of the phrases above – that use the word in the plural form (*dogs, books, pears*).
- Now write three short sentences using the words in the singular with a possessive apostrophe (*dog's, book's, pear's*).
- Is the difference in meaning clear? Reflect on how the context and look of the word can help us comprehend the intended meaning.

The plural -s and possessive apostrophe can also be combined to show belonging. Consider the changing meaning over the following sentences:

(1) The cats sat on the mat.

(2) The cat's mat was soft and comfortable.

(3) The cats' mat was soft and comfortable.

In the first sentence there is more than one cat. In the second sentence the mat belongs to a single cat; in the third, the mat belongs to all of the cats. If the text had already referred to many cats it would seem strange if only one of them owned the mat on which they were sat, so it would make more sense to the reader to link sentences 1 and 3.

An added complication comes when we try to distinguish between the use of a possessive apostrophe with (1) singular words ending in -s and (2) words that are plural (Table 8.1).

Table 8.1 Apostrophes for singular and plural

Singular	Singular with possessive apostrophe	Plural	Plural with possessive apostrophe
Class	Class's	Classes	Classes'
Boss	Boss's	Bosses	Bosses'
Bus	Bus's	Buses	Buses'

The words in the box are all spoken the same way: it is only possible to distinguish their meaning through context when heard, but when written, their meaning is made clear by the use of the apostrophe and -s (or -es in this case).

How children learn about the plural and possessive -s

Most of the grammar teaching you will do in English relates to syntax (the way sentences are structured) but when teaching about the use of possessive apostrophes the focus is on the morphology (the way words are structured). Crystal (1988, p227) points out that English has relatively few suffixes that act as inflections, *noun plural* and *genitive -'s* being two of them.

The concepts needed in order to understand the grammatical differences should all be in place by Year 4. Children should be familiar with singular and plural nouns; they should also be confident in their use of apostrophes to show contractions. Use of apostrophes to show belonging (possessive apostrophes) is also prior learning that is necessary in order to be able to explore grammatical difference.

Although the genitive -'s mainly refers to belonging, it should be noted that it also indicates origin, description, measure and role. When you write 'a winter's evening' or

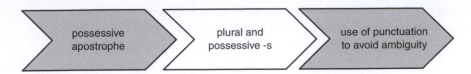

Figure 8.2 Learning plural and possessive -s

'a week's holiday' it can be hard to explain why the apostrophe is necessary because it is difficult to think of a season or time period owning something. A good explanation of the different uses of the genitive case can be found on pp124–125 of *Rediscover Grammar* (Crystal, 1988).

Teaching your class: Year 4

It is possible to look at the grammatical difference between the use of the plural -s and the possessive -s in a range of text types. However, the use of small sections of prose texts sometimes makes the learning feel disjointed. Poetry offers a way of looking at particular features of writing in a full text rather than extracts, which can make it feel more purposeful; it is also a great way of exploring language for effect.

Context

This Year 4 class have had the poem *The Listeners* by Walter De La Mare (**http://www.poemhunter.com/poem/the-listeners/**) read to them as part of their learning about narrative poetry. They have discussed who the character of the Traveller might be, written letters from the Traveller's viewpoint in order to present reasons for his visit and collected pictures (as homework) of buildings that they feel could be the one described in the poem. They have also done a brief analysis of the text structure to identify the rhyme scheme and syllable pattern used.

Learning objectives

- To use the possessive apostrophe with plural nouns.

- To identify the grammatical difference between plural and possessive -s.

> **Commentary**
>
> The objectives here fit within the lesson but are not the only things being taught: the unit itself is about writing effective narrative poetry. The lesson will offer an opportunity to apply a grammatical feature accurately (the genitive case) and will encourage analysis of the effect.

Lesson opener: Is it mine?

Using flashcards or objects ask the children to identify the owner of a range of items. Model the first couple, for example, a whiteboard pen and a tiara. On whiteboards the children write who owns the object (for example, a teacher/you; a princess/queen). Do this for five more objects or pictures.

In talk partners ask children to discuss the ways we show who owns an object in a sentence for one minute. Then ask them to choose an object from the items already seen and put it into a short sentence, for example:

> The queen wore *her* tiara. (Possessive pronoun)

> The teacher's whiteboard pen didn't work. (Possessive apostrophe)

> **Commentary**
>
> • The pace of this activity should be swift as it is encouraging children to recall prior learning rather than teaching new skills.

Then hand out a table similar to Table 8.2.

Table 8.2 Possessive apostrophe exercise

the bravery of the explorer	
the chatter of the children	
the stillness of the leaves	

Explain you want the pupils to practise using the possessive apostrophe by redrafting each of the phrases in a different order; you can model an example for them if necessary, e.g. *the song of the bird – the bird's song.* Briefly summarise the way that different words and punctuation can help us see what objects and attributes belong to someone or something.

> **Commentary**
>
> The final phrase, 'the stillness of the leaves', demonstrates how the plural does not need an extra -s, just an apostrophe. It is worth modelling errors on the board to unpick how odd it would sound if it was written/read as 'leaves's'. This will help children remember the different purposes of the -s and the apostrophe.

Main lesson

Introduction

Share with the pupils a version of *The Listeners* by Walter De La Mare (there are multimodal versions available on YouTube if you feel this is appropriate or you do not feel confident reading the poem aloud). They should have paper copies they have been using to support previous learning, so could be encouraged to read along. Return to the title: *The Listeners*. Why do they think the writer chose to call it this instead of *The Traveller*? Discuss this for one minute using talk partners.

Commentary

It is important that the pupils understand they can only infer their ideas here: there is no definitive answer, but they are hypothesising about the author's intent.

Ask for three suggestions which might explain the title. For each, ask the pair to 'Tell me' why they have reached their hypothesis.

Commentary

In Aidan Chambers' book *Tell Me: Children, Reading and Talk* (first published in 1993) he details the development of the 'Tell me' approach, which has influenced educational professionals and teaching strategies in recent years. It is worth reading up on this approach to help you use it effectively, as it contains guidance about the reading environment which will support your teaching.

Explain that today the pupils will be writing from the point of view of the Listeners. They will have many decisions to make as the omniscient narrator (the narrator as all-seeing, rather than narrator as one of the characters).

Commentary

It is important that they don't confuse point of view with author's voice. In the original poem the narrative is told from the Traveller's point of view, but only the words he speaks are in the first person; the rest of the text is in the third person.

In order to scaffold the task for some of the pupils you may wish to provide a writing frame which provides support for the use of rhyme or reminders of the syllable pattern. The syllable pattern is not rigid, but is somewhere between 10 and 12 for odd-numbered lines and 7 syllables for even-numbered lines, so you could provide a frame that indicates where the shorter lines appear (Figure 8.3).

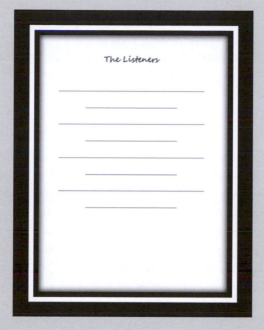

Figure 8.3   Writing frame

Critical questions to ask pupils:

- How will the reader know that there is more than one Listener?

- What descriptions or roles are being applied to the Listeners in your text?

Commentary

They need to consider the actions of the group rather than the individual, and make this clear in their writing by remembering to use the plural. The Listeners should be treated as a collective, so roles, actions and descriptions should be applied to them all.

Practical application

The children then draft their ideas for their version of the poem (eight lines in length) using the prompts and visual stimulus material gathered as part of previous activities. They will need to make careful vocabulary choices to ensure they can match the A/B/C/B rhyme scheme, and begin to make precise use of punctuation to guide the reader.

Commentary

During this section of the lesson the focus is on the content of the poem, but the children should be encouraged to see accurate use of punctuation and structure as integral to the process and not an afterthought to be saved for the proof-reading stage. It is much easier to apply learned techniques at the point of drafting than to add them in later. Teaching children how to plan effectively can support this process as they can get their ideas down quickly in plan form and then take more care over each draft: a plan should not be the same as a first draft.

Plenary

Play 'Pass the Parcel Peer Review': play a piece of music (or even the multimodal reading of the original poem if a YouTube clip was used for the introduction) and ask the pupils to pass their poems around the class. When the music/clip is halted they must read the text in front of them and identify an example of the correct use of the rhyme scheme, circling/highlighting it and annotating with the abbreviation RS for rhyme scheme. Play the clip again for the children to pass the poems on: this time when the music stops they need to identify the way the writer has used the syllable pattern by counting the syllables in the first four lines and marking the number at the beginning of each line. Play the music again, and when the clip stops ask them to identify any use of the possessive apostrophe with the plural noun (most likely *Listeners'*). Ask for examples of effective phrases which demonstrate appropriate use of the apostrophe, possibly in response to an element of the original poem. For example, where De La Mare wrote:

> *And a bird flew up out of the turret,*
>
> *Above the Traveller's head:*

the children may have responded with something like:

> *At the flight of the bird the Listeners' ears*
>
> *Pricked at the sound of their wings;*

Use a visualiser if possible to show the children examples and analyse how the punctuation helps us understand that the Traveller is alone while the Listeners are not.

Commentary

By using 'Pass the Parcel Peer Review' for the plenary you are enabling children to see several examples of their peers' writing while sharing out the responsibility for feedback. This can get around issues such as perceived favouritism amongst friends, for example, as it is entirely random.

By focusing the feedback on the key aspects of structure and use of punctuation at this point you are not offering the opportunity to criticise the children's ideas; self-reflection on the content can be done in a subsequent lesson.

Assessment (measuring achievement)

Assessment for learning

There are aspects of learning you will need to be sure the children have experienced and understood that are not a part of the lesson detailed above, for example the other uses of the apostrophe (to indicate contractions or omissions). It is important that they are clear what an apostrophe is and on the difference between omission and possession.

- The starter activity will enable you to assess the children's level of understanding regarding the use of possessive apostrophes.
- Identify the way apostrophes are used in the original poem to model the use of the genitive case with singular nouns.

Assessment at the point of learning

The lesson offers several checkpoint opportunities for you to monitor the application of learning and address misconceptions.

- The use of whiteboards enables you to check all pupils have remembered the conventions of plurals and apostrophes.
- During the drafting process, monitor the pupils' use of punctuation when writing about the Listeners. Make a note of any children who may need further intervention, and provide guided support (either from you as the teacher or a teaching assistant) during this section of the lesson for those who need it as part of differentiation.

Assessment of learning

The correct application of the possessive apostrophe and the plural -s will demonstrate children's ability to meet the key objective, which is:

- To use the possessive apostrophe accurately in words with regular plurals (for example, girls', boys') and in words with irregular plurals (for example, children's).

It will also indicate their understanding of the grammatical difference between the different -s morphemes. Any errors in the use of the genitive case or -s as a morpheme in the drafts of the poems need to be analysed to see if they are indicators of an underlying misconception or just mistakes through carelessness.

Challenges

- Prior learning. If pupils have not consolidated their understanding of singular and plural nouns as well as the use of the possessive apostrophe they will find it difficult to recognise how the two work together.

- Reluctant writers/poor planners. Pupils who rush to finish tasks rather than considering the audience and purpose are more likely to make mistakes in the application of punctuation for grammatical meaning. Teaching children to use a range of planning formats and allowing them to choose the one that works for them for each task can help them consider their ideas more carefully; also, by making the use of punctuation part of the explicit success criteria you will encourage them to consider it during the writing rather than add it afterwards.

Application of learning

Links to other areas of the curriculum

The use of the possessive apostrophe with plural nouns, and the ability to recognise and understand the different grammatical uses of -s, applies across the curriculum and thus does not lend itself to any particular subject area. It is just as likely to feature in non-fiction text types as in narrative, drama or poetry.

Next lesson

Precise use of punctuation, especially those marks that look similar but have different uses, can be commented on each lesson until new uses are embedded. A punctuation display board or table mat which provides definitions and examples of usage can be used for reference and will scaffold those working towards independence. The issue with punctuation is not, have the children been taught it? but *have they learned it?* Providing opportunities for review and analysis, and making the use of punctuation a focus of the success criteria or assessment framework which is shared with the children will help them become familiar with correct usage.

Learning outcomes review

The use of possessive apostrophes with regular plural nouns may seem simple to apply but unless the morphemic differences are understood it can appear arbitrary to learners. In this chapter we have explored one possible lesson where this aspect of morphology and punctuation can be the focus, but until errors are few and far between in independent writing tasks you may need to discuss it explicitly across a range of texts.

Points to consider

- How might you personalise the learning of the genitive case for your class?
- What opportunities do you provide for children to annotate their own texts as well as the writing of others (both peer and published) in order to identify grammatical features? Is it an integral part of your teaching and the children's learning?

Further reading

Chambers, A. (2011) *Tell Me: Children, Reading and Talk with The Reading Environment.* Stroud: Thimble Press.

A compendium of two key texts by Aidan Chambers. Both books provide clear guidance on how to develop a language and text-rich environment with details of the research and exploration that led to Chambers' conclusions.

Pearson Education (2013) *Grammar and Spelling Bug: Unit 5 Possessive-Apostrophes.* Pearson.

Pearson have developed their literacy 'bug' series to include updated grammar and spelling materials. There are free units for each age phase available on their website: the possessive apostrophe unit can be found at: **www.pearsonschoolsandfecolleges.co.uk/Primary/GlobalPages/GSBugFreeUnit/ GrammarandSpellingBugFreeUnitYears3-4.aspx**

Reedy, D. and Bearne, E. (2013) *Teaching Grammar Effectively in Primary Schools.* UKLA.

Section 3 of this book contains some activities labelled 'Quick + Easy' which provide ideas for teaching about the possessive -s and apostrophes.

References

Chambers, A. (2011) *Tell Me: Children, Reading and Talk with The Reading Environment*. Stroud: Thimble Press.

Crystal, D. (1988) *Rediscover Grammar*. Harlow: Longman.

Department for Education (DfE) (2013) *The National Curriculum in England: Framework Document*. London: DfE.

Chapter 9

Year 5: Teaching modal verbs

Learning outcomes

In this chapter, you will look at how to teach modal verbs. You will explore what children need to know in order to use them correctly and what you need to know in order to teach them effectively. You will also consider ways in which you can develop children's understanding of how to use them to enhance their writing.

This chapter will allow you to achieve the following outcomes:

- develop an understanding of what children need to know about modal verbs;
- develop an understanding of the use of modal verbs to enhance writing;
- have a greater awareness of some of the challenges you may face when teaching modal verbs;
- become more confident in your approach to teaching modal verbs.

Teachers' Standards

Working through this chapter will help you meet the following standards:

3. Demonstrate good subject and curriculum knowledge.
4. Plan and teach well-structured lessons.
5. Adapt teaching to respond to the strengths and needs of all pupils.
6. Make accurate and productive use of assessment.

Links to the National Curriculum

Upper Key Stage 2 statutory requirement

Years 5 and 6
Pupils should be taught to:

- draft and write by:

  ✓ selecting appropriate grammar and vocabulary, understanding how such choices can change and enhance meaning

- evaluate and edit by:
  - ✓ assessing the effectiveness of their own and others' writing
  - ✓ proposing changes to vocabulary, grammar and punctuation to enhance effects and clarify meaning
  - ✓ ensuring the consistent and correct use of tense throughout a piece of writing

- develop their understanding of the concepts set out in Appendix 2 by:
  - ✓ using modal verbs or adverbs to indicate degrees of possibility

- use and understand the grammatical terminology in Appendix 2 accurately and appropriately in discussing their writing and reading.

(DfE, 2013)

Key focus: Using modal verbs

You may think that a verb is simply a 'doing word'. However, as discussed in the chapters on verb tenses, they are more than mere 'doing' words. A verb describes an action, an occurrence or a state of being. Verbs can change the whole tone of a text. Consider the difference between someone 'creeping' into a room and someone 'charging' into a room. The verb conveys meaning and intent in this instance.

Within a clause, the verb element consists of one or more verbs which make up the verb phrase. There are two main types of verb that can occur within a verb phrase:

- The *main verb*, which indicates meaning, for example:

  read   swim   argue   wonder   like

  He *jumped* into the pool.
  She *enjoyed* the ice cream.

- The *auxiliary verb*, which 'helps' the main verb by expressing shades of meaning. There are many main verbs but only a few auxiliary verbs:

  be do have can could may might must shall should will would

  She *must* be finished by now.
  They *might* arrive this afternoon.
  I *have* eaten it.

The auxiliary verbs, *be*, *do* and *have* can also act as main verbs within a clause as they possess a full range of verb forms:

  The coat *has* a green hood.
  The coats *have* green hoods.
  The coat *had* a green hood.

The remaining auxiliary verbs are known as *modal verbs* and cannot be used as main verbs as they do not have a full range of forms. *Mighting* and *shoulding* do not exist as a verb form although *doing*, *being* and *having* are acceptable forms.

Activity

Identify the main verb and the auxiliary verb in the following sentences. Some may have more than one auxiliary verb.

Can you identify which are modal auxiliary verbs?

I might eat that sandwich later.

She was so happy.

They promised I could attend the ceremony next week.

He could see for miles.

I have a new dress to wear for the party.

She is a beautiful cat.

Please may I leave the table?

Would you be able to help me with my shopping?

He ran quickly down the stairs.

He should have forgiven him before now.

The statutory appendix for grammar and punctuation included in the National Curriculum for 2014 provides an overview of the specific types of verbs that should be included in teaching the programmes of study. One such type is *modal verb*. Modal verbs are auxiliary verbs referring to events that may potentially happen rather than events that have taken place. They express shades of meaning and can enhance children's writing by allowing them to express degrees of probability, certainty, necessity, obligation and volition. For many years, the mark schemes for the Year 6 End of Key Stage 2 (SAT) papers have specifically referred to the inclusion of modal verbs in the writing task, thus marks were awarded for their use within the text. The previous marking schemes for the End of Key Stage 2 longer writing task refer specifically to the modal verbs 'could' and 'should' but you need to be aware of the others and how you can teach children to use them appropriately within their writing.

How children learn about modal verbs

Children need to develop the ability to use modal verbs so that they can express degrees of possibility, probability, willingness, necessity, certainty and obligation within their written texts. Using modal verbs will enable children to make predictions, to speculate and to make deductions which all contribute to the level of sophistication within their writing. Children should already be familiar with the function of a verb within a clause from the work they have done in Year 2 and will have built upon this by exploring verb tenses in Year 3. They should understand the function of a verb (although may need reminding that it is not simply a 'doing' word) and will probably be able to talk about the past, present and future tense of verbs as this is closely linked to the work that they may have undertaken on spelling. In Year 3, pupils are required to know about the use of the present perfect form of verbs in addition to the simple past, for example, *he has been working hard to pass his exams* as opposed to *he worked hard to pass his exams.* As a teacher, you will need to know what these terms mean. If you are confident in your knowledge and use of grammatical features, you will be able to use the terms correctly with the children and once children have been introduced to the correct terminology, they will have a common language through which to talk about usage. As discussed in the second chapter, one of the main principles underpinning Debra Myhill's study into the impact of embedded grammar teaching on pupils' writing was the use of a grammatical metalanguage which was used confidently by teachers and pupils (Myhill et al., 2011). This is defined as a *language about language* (DfE, 2013, p15) in the 2014 National Curriculum.

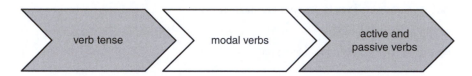

Figure 9.1   Learning about modal verbs

Exposure to modal verbs in children's reading will provide opportunities for them to discuss meaning and they will become more confident when commenting upon the overall effect that these create within a text. It is important that you explore this with children so that they are equipped to choose appropriate modal verbs to illustrate precise meaning clearly. In the sentence, *He could have made a run for it*, why has the author chosen to include *could* when commenting upon the character's actions? How would this change the meaning of the sentence if the author had written: *He made a run for it*? What does it tell us about the character? Encourage children to use modal verbs in their own writing to suggest possibility, probability and certainty.

Teaching your class: Year 5

The following lesson is intended as a starting point for teaching your Year 5 class and will provide guidance on teaching modal verbs within the context of a wider Literacy framework rather than through the use of grammar exercises. You may choose to use some or the entire lesson to help children begin to understand how to use modal verbs to improve their writing.

Context

The pupils in Year 5 have recently completed work on persuasive texts and are able to employ a range of persuasive devices, including rhetorical questions, emotional language, exaggeration and repetition. They have constructed adverts for new products that they have presented to some local business people in an attempt to persuade them to manufacture their product. To practise writing persuasive letters, they have written letters to the local council asking them to build a skateboard ramp in the local park. In both cases, the children had a purpose for their work and received feedback indicating the success of their persuasive writing. They are now exploring the use of modal verbs in texts to suggest shades of meaning and degrees of certainty.

Learning objectives

- To explore the functions of modal verbs.

- To be able to explain how changing the modal verb can change the meaning of the sentence.

- To use modal verbs accurately to convey meaning.

> **Commentary**
>
> The learning objective focuses upon what modal verbs do to modify main verbs and how they can subtly alter the intention of the writer to a greater or lesser degree. It is important that children can use them correctly to change the tone of their writing, indicating possibility, certainty or necessity. In this case, the learning objectives not only refer to the subject knowledge required, but also allude to the application of skills when writing. If children can explain how the use of various modal verbs can alter the meaning of a sentence, they are demonstrating an understanding of how modal verbs work. Through the use of precise learning objectives together with comprehensive success criteria, children will be able to identify what it is they need to address in their next piece of work so that they continue to progress their learning.

Starter: Shades of meaning

Arrange the children into groups of four or five and hand them an envelope containing sentences that include modal verbs. You could also use tablets or laptops and ask the children to move the sentences on the screen. Ask the children to order them according to certainty of outcome and highlight the particular words or phrases that give an indication of possibility.

> Examples may include:
>
> Tom should defeat the dragon.
>
> Tom might defeat the dragon.
>
> Tom will defeat the dragon.
>
> (Continued)

(Continued)

Sentences may be tailored to reflect your current topic or class reading book so that the children are able to relate possibilities to particular characters when they are making their decisions. Through discussion, examine the function of modal verbs within the sentences and clarify any misconceptions. This will provide an opportunity to assess the children's current levels of understanding. Note children who readily identify modal verbs and understand how they subtly change the meaning of the sentence; you can do this through discussion with the groups or by directing a teaching assistant to make a note of children who can explain why the sentences are different. These children would benefit from a greater level of challenge as a guided group during the main part of the session. Introduce the term modal verb so that the children are able to discuss the sentences using the correct terminology. Write the nine most common modal auxiliary verbs on the whiteboard or add them to your working wall.

Main lesson

Introduction

Show the class a plain cardboard box containing a pair of trainers and explain that a local business is about to manufacture these trainers and we have the only prototype. We need to plan a marketing strategy to persuade people that these are the greatest trainers on earth. Alternatively, you could use a new soft drink, an item of clothing or a new breakfast cereal. Try relating the product to your class topic or the interests of your class. You could even invite a local business in to talk to the children or 'mock up' a letter from a business. Another option is to ask someone to act in role to explain the task to the children. You may also want to consider asking someone to act as an expert (for example, the chief executive officer of a company) to communicate the task by emailing a video clip. Consider how best to engage the children in your class.

How you wish to introduce this task will depend upon your class and their experiences of writing in role. The added dimension of an 'expert' requesting the advert helps to set the task within a real context and provides a purpose for the written work. There is also no reason why you couldn't ask the children to produce a video campaign rather than a written outcome using appropriate and familiar software; just remember that this lesson should have a grammar focus rather than a technical computing focus.

Explain that the use of modal verbs will be very important in the campaign and they must produce an advert to persuade people to buy the product. You may want to suggest children work in pairs or individually depending on the needs of your class.

Begin by showing the children an advert that you have written with sentences containing modal verbs. Invite discussion and ask for clarification. Challenge the more able by asking them to suggest alternative sentences. Ask them: which would be more effective? Why?

Show the children your advert, which contains sentences such as:

These trainers might be the best thing you ever buy.

These trainers may change your life.

You will be able to run faster, jump higher, leap further.

You should buy them before they are sold out.

Ask the children to choose the most effective sentence and give reasons for their choice. You may want to invite them to discuss this with a talk partner

(Continued)

(Continued)

first and write their reasons on a mini-whiteboard or you could work with a targeted group asking questions to promote discussion.

To challenge the more able pupils, you could ask them to work in pairs to write alternative sentences on whiteboards or type them on tablets. Ask children to highlight the modal verb used so that you can assess their level of understanding. Encourage children to justify their choice of modal verb in order to assess understanding.

During this part of the lesson, you should be assessing knowledge and understanding so that you can ensure all children make progress through support and challenge as appropriate.

Choose sentences written by the children that demonstrate the effective use of modal verbs to add to the class working wall to act as good examples. You will need to explain why they are effective and how a sentence such as *You will be the envy of your friends* is more powerful than *You might be the envy of your friends* when attempting to persuade people to buy your product.

Critical questions to ask pupils:

- Substitute your modal verb for an alternative. Does it still have the same meaning?

- How has it changed the meaning of the sentence?

- Can you explain your choice of modal verb to a partner?

- Does your sentence read well and make sense? Compare with examples on the working wall.

Practical application

Children can design their advert using modal verbs that have a particular function for this genre of writing. You will need to consider the use of scaffolds and prompts to support some children. You may want to ask some children to record their sentences using Easi-Speak microphones or video cameras so that they are less constrained by the transcriptional skills necessary to produce a written advert. More able children may benefit from completing a storyboard for a TV advert or writing a letter to a company asking them to stock the trainers.

Application of learning may run across a number of lessons and could easily form the basis of a cross-curricular topic on business enterprise. Children are applying their knowledge of modal verbs in a particular context and developing an understanding of how they can deliberately manipulate texts to change meaning.

Plenary

In pairs, children need to organise themselves so that one is acting as a marketing expert and one is a member of the public. The children must role play the conversation using sentences containing modal verbs. Pupils can give feedback to their partners on how their choice of phrases influenced their decision to buy the product. Write their most effective phrase on a sticky note and attach it to the front of their book.

> By writing what they consider to be the most effective phrase containing a modal verb, the children are providing you with a means of assessing understanding. Not only will individual pupils be able to reflect upon their learning, you will be able to identify those children requiring further support or challenge in subsequent lessons.

Assessment (measuring achievement)

Assessment for learning

- The starter activity in this lesson allows you to assess prior knowledge. The children may not necessarily be aware that they are specifically using modal verbs but may be able to use them correctly to indicate shades of meaning.

- You may want to explore the use of these verbs during guided reading, asking children to explain why the author has chosen to employ that particular verb. This will also provide opportunities to discuss alternatives and assess how much children know about their function.

- Ask the children to compose sentences containing each of the nine main modal verbs: can, could, may, might, must, shall, should, will, would. How does it change the intention of the character? Can they order them on a continuum from possible to probable to certain?

Assessment at the point of learning

- Ensure that any teaching assistants or adults working within your lesson are aware of what constitutes learning in terms of modal verb use. When they see children using modal verbs correctly or demonstrating their understanding through careful explanation of choice, ask them to record this on a sticky note or in a designated book. In this way, you will be able to address individual learning throughout the course of the lesson.

- When you are working with a guided group, challenge children by asking the critical questions suggested above. You will be able to assess their learning by evaluating the answers they give and address misconceptions in order to clarify understanding.

Can they explain why they should include *might* rather than *will*? How does this change the meaning of the sentence? Does it contribute to the effectiveness of the text?

Can they explain why? Do they understand the difference between *shall* and *should*? All of these questions will need to be explored if you are to ensure that every child achieves the learning objectives for this particular lesson.

Assessment of learning

When marking the children's work, you will need to consider the following questions:

- Have the pupils demonstrated accurate use of modal verbs?

- Have pupils identified modal verbs correctly within the text?

- Have the pupils deliberately chosen a modal verb that shows intent?

- To what extent have the pupils persuaded you to purchase the product?

Note how children use modal verbs in other curriculum subjects and when writing different types of text.

Challenges

- Children will need to understand how a verb operates within a clause. Before asking children to identify modal auxiliary verbs, make sure that they possess the necessary understanding of main verbs.

- There is a tendency for some children to write *he could of* instead of *he could have* as this is what they hear in conversation. It might be appropriate to spend some time explaining this to your class so as to avoid this grammatical inconsistency.

- Pupils for whom English is an additional language (EAL) need to develop the ability to use modal verbs to express a greater range of possibilities. The subtleties in meaning will need to be given explicit attention and demonstrated in detail, particularly for lower-achieving EAL writers. This could be done through drama, speaking and listening activities or through discussion around common dilemmas, for example, *what would you do if. . .?*

Application of learning

Links to other areas of the curriculum

Modal verbs allow the writer to qualify statements and make judgements. They indicate precise meaning and clarify intent. They are particularly prevalent in persuasion and argument-based texts but can also feature heavily in science investigations which demand a degree of prediction and speculation. You may wish to reinforce the use of modal verbs when covering the following:

- Science: making predictions, writing up conclusions;

- PSHE: when discussing moral dilemmas and making suggestions as to how we might act during specific situations;

- Drama: what might the character do? What should he do? Justifying behaviour;

- DT: when formulating instructions and writing explanations.

Next lesson

One of the main challenges you will face is ensuring that the children in your class use modal verbs correctly and consistently when it is not the main focus of the lesson. How can we achieve this successfully? Remind children of the use of modal verbs when approaching other genres of writing. When writing a story, use modal verbs to suggest the character's intention and hint at what might happen next. Explore an author's use of modal verbs when examining a character's actions during guided reading. What should Mary do upon discovering the secret garden? What will Harry Potter do to protect his friends? Books such as Liz Pichon's *Tom Gates* series, *Skellig* by David Almond and *Stormbreaker* by Anthony Horowitz provide children with the opportunity to discuss the use of modal verbs when exploring characters' motives and actions. Ensure that children are continuing to use modal verbs correctly and include them as part of success criteria if appropriate.

Learning outcomes review

In this chapter you have explored the use of modal verbs within texts and how to begin to teach them effectively within a Literacy lesson. You should now feel more confident in your approach to teaching children how to use modal verbs and in addressing some of the challenges that may arise. You should also have ideas for working with children to use modal verbs to express subtleties of possibility and probability in order to enhance the text.

The lesson plan presented acts as a starting point for teaching modal verbs to a class of Year 5 children and the commentary offers an explanation as to the pedagogies adopted. However, you will probably want to adapt the lesson plan to suit the needs and interests of your own class.

Points to consider

- How might you challenge the more able pupils to take risks in their writing and use modal verbs to express precise meaning?
- Can you adapt the lesson idea to teach other year groups about verbs?
- Would you be able to teach other aspects of grammatical knowledge using a similar structure?

Further reading

Cameron, L. and Besser, S. (2004) *Writing in English as an Additional Language at Key Stage 2.* Nottingham: DfES.

This document presents research conducted by Professor Lynne Cameron and Dr Sharon Besser, investigating grammatical features presenting particular challenges for pupils learning EAL.

Crystal, D. (2004) *Rediscover Grammar.* Essex: Pearson Education.

Chapter 26 looks specifically at the use of modal verbs and gives examples to clarify meaning. It is also very good for defining grammatical terms and provides excellent examples of usage.

Department for Children, Schools and Families (DCSF) (2009) *Support for Spelling*. London: DCSF.

This is a useful document to aid subject knowledge and it also includes some particularly effective ways in which to teach verbs.

Department for Education and Skills (DfES) (2006) *Excellence and Enjoyment: Learning and Teaching for Bilingual Children in the Primary Years, Unit 2. Creating the Learning Culture: Making It Work in the Classroom*. London: DfES.

This document is particularly helpful when working with pupils with EAL as it contains support materials to assist in the teaching of writing.

References

Almond, D. (1998) *Skellig*. London: Hodder.

Department for Education (DfE) (2013) *The National Curriculum in England: Framework Document*. London: DfE.

Horowitz, A. (2003) *Stormbreaker*. London: Walker Books.

Myhill, D., Jones, S., Lines, H. and Watson, A. (2011) Re-thinking grammar: the impact of embedded grammar teaching on students' writing and students' metalinguistic understanding. *Research Papers in Education*, 27 (2): 139–166.

Pichon, L. (2011–2013). *Tom Gates* series. London: Scholastic.

Chapter 10

Year 5: Teaching expanded noun phrases

Learning outcomes

This chapter provides some practical examples of strategies and resources to teach expanded noun phrases within the context of a Literacy lesson and explores what you need to know in order to teach them effectively.

This chapter will allow you to achieve the following outcomes:

- develop your knowledge of expanded noun phrases;
- understand how expanded noun phrases can improve clarity of writing;
- have a greater understanding of how to teach expanded noun phrases.

Teachers' Standards

Working through this chapter will help you meet the following standards:

3. Demonstrate good subject and curriculum knowledge.
4. Plan and teach well-structured lessons.
5. Adapt teaching to respond to the strengths and needs of all pupils.

Links to the National Curriculum

Upper Key Stage 2 statutory requirement

Years 5 and 6
Pupils should be taught to:

- plan their writing by:

  ✓ identifying the audience for and purpose of the writing, selecting the appropriate form and using other similar writing as models for their own

- draft and write by:

  ✓ selecting appropriate grammar and vocabulary, understanding how such choices can change and enhance meaning

- evaluate and edit by:

  ✓ assessing the effectiveness of their own and others' writing
  ✓ proposing changes to vocabulary, grammar and punctuation to enhance effects and clarify meaning

- develop their understanding of the concepts set out in Appendix 2 by:

  ✓ using expanded noun phrases to convey complicated information concisely

- use and understand the grammatical terminology in Appendix 2 accurately and appropriately in discussing their writing and reading.

(DfE, 2013)

Key focus: Using expanded noun phrases

You may be forgiven for thinking that a noun phrase is one of the simpler grammatical devices that can be employed in your writing. However, it is not simply a matter of adding an adjective to a noun in order to create a noun phrase. Noun phrases and extended noun phrases are used to enrich writing and to add extra information which serves to build a clear picture in the reader's mind. Compare these two sentences:

The sun shone.
The midday sun beat down heavily on the dry, dusty road.

Consider how the extra information in the second sentence has added detail for the reader. Used effectively, the expanded noun phrase can shape the landscape of the text and enhance the tone of the writing. However, if overused or employed incorrectly, the writing may become stilted and too reliant on description alone. It is therefore imperative that you teach your children to use noun phrases to enrich the text and improve the quality of their writing.

The National Curriculum for 2014 stipulates that pupils need to be able to include noun phrases that not only add information but do so in a concise manner. Therefore, it is much more than the inclusion of strings of adjectives and adverbs. The whole point of a noun phrase is that it conveys complex and detailed information in an efficient yet meaningful manner. To be able to teach children about expanded noun phrases, you need to understand how a noun works within a sentence and how you can construct sentences effectively using noun phrases and expanded noun phrases.

Let us start with the *noun* as it forms the basis of a noun phrase. Nouns are words which refer to people, places, objects and ideas. There are different types of nouns, which may be divided as shown in Figure 10.1.

A *noun phrase* is a string of words centred on a single noun. This noun is known as the head. In its simplest form, it consists of the noun but some noun phrases contain long

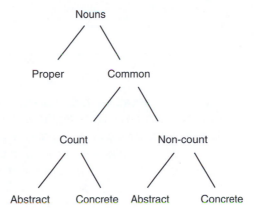

Figure 10.1   Different types of nouns

and complex strings of words which convey a great deal of extra information and are known as *expanded noun phrases*. In the example below, each sentence contains a noun phrase. The main noun or head is underlined in each instance:

<u>Books</u>	are great.
<u>The books</u>	are great.
<u>The story books</u>	are great.
<u>The story books in the library</u>	are great.

You can therefore see that each sentence, despite the inclusion of extra words, is actually about the same thing. One of the ways in which you can check to see if it is a noun phrase is to replace the noun phrase with a pronoun. Does it still make sense if we write *they are interesting?* Yes it does, but it is not nearly as interesting for the reader.

Noun phrases usually consist of the following: determiners, premodifiers (words before the noun), the head word and postmodifiers (words after the noun). See the examples in Table 10.1.

Table 10.1   Different parts of noun phrases

Determiners	Premodifiers	Head word	Postmodifiers
the	giant	tree	in the forest
a	wonderful	cup	of tea
the two	young	children	from down the road

Activity

1. Can you identify the noun phrases in the passage below, taken from Michael Morpurgo's short story, *The Giant's Necklace?*

   Boat Cove just below Zennor Head was the beach they had found and occupied. Every year for as long as Cherry could remember they had rented the same granite cottage, set back in the fields below the Eagle's Nest and every year they came to the same beach because no one else did. In two weeks not another soul had ventured down the winding track through the bracken from the coastal path. It was a long climb down and a very much longer one up. The beach itself was almost hidden from the path that ran along the cliff top a hundred feet above. It was private and perfect and theirs. The boys swam amongst the rocks, diving and snorkelling for hours on end. Her mother and father would sit side by side on stripy deck chairs.

2. Can you expand these noun phrases by adding a determiner, premodifier and postmodifier?

   Lakes are beautiful.

   The car sped down the road.

   The child fell over.

   The cat ran along the wall.

3. Can you identify the head of the noun phrase in the examples above?

How children learn about expanded noun phrases

A noun phrase is a word or group of words that acts in the same way as a noun. They clarify detail for the reader and can focus attention through the use of precise and specific description. Pupils need to know how to use premodifiers and postmodifiers to expand a noun phrase, building upon work completed in lower Key Stage 2. Most children should be able to identify a single noun within a phrase and expand noun phrases for description by adding adjectives, for example, *the clear blue sea.* They may also be confident to add a prepositional phrase after the noun, for example, *the red ball in the garden*. In Year 4, pupils are expected to expand noun phrases by adding modifying adjectives, nouns and prepositional phrases, thus creating a more complex and detailed sentence, for example, *the angry little boy with a frown on his face* . . . The next step for children would be to write expanded noun phrases, choosing from the most appropriate and effective range of modifiers in order to convey detailed information to the reader. Consider the two examples below:

The beach was sandy. It stretched on for miles. It was covered in seaweed. The seaweed was green.

The sandy beach, which seemed to stretch for miles, was covered in a carpet of green seaweed.

In the first example, the writing seems rather stilted. Repetition of the pronoun 'it' and use of full stops interrupts the flow of the text. The second sentence suggests a more mature style of writing and manages to convey a great deal of information in one complete sentence. Therefore, you can see how children learn about expanded noun phrases as part of the learning continuum in order to focus the reader's attention by conveying information in a rather more economical manner.

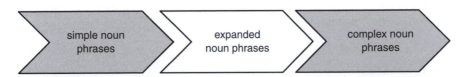

Figure 10.2   Learning about noun phrases

Remember that it is not simply a matter of teaching children the correct grammatical terms; it is important that you discuss word and sentence choices so that they are able to use noun phrases that convey effective and powerful description. Shared writing is a powerful tool for demonstrating the thinking behind a text. Show the children how the inclusion of an expanded noun phrase can improve the flow of their writing. Read it aloud together to get a feel for the effect it creates. Experiment with building up a noun phrase, each child contributing to the sentence. Create long and complex nonsense sentences, extending vocabulary choices and justifying meaning. Highlight particularly vivid noun phrases in children's books. How has the author created the picture in our heads? You may want to share books such as Michael Morpurgo's *Kensuke's Kingdom*, *The Secret Garden* by Frances Hodgson Burnett and the Harry Potter books, which will provide excellent examples when teaching children about expanded noun phrases.

Teaching your class: Year 5

The following lesson suggests some ways in which you can teach expanded noun phrases to a Year 5 class and outlines a framework within which to work in order to structure your lesson. It may act as a single lesson or be adapted as a series of lessons depending upon the needs of your class. Incorporate the interests of your own class so that you are making the teaching meaningful and relevant to their experiences.

Context

For the purpose of this lesson, the pupils in Year 5 have spent some time examining description in narrative through shared and guided reading. They have identified powerful verbs and effective adjectives and explored how the use of adverbials can convey a particular mood. There are many examples on the working wall and the children have been encouraged to use descriptive devices in their written work over the past few weeks. Their topic is 'The Great Outdoors' and they are midway through a poetry unit of work in their Literacy lessons, culminating in a class assembly at the end of term. The class teacher is now extending their knowledge of noun phrases by teaching them how to write and employ expanded noun phrases effectively.

Learning objectives

- To identify expanded noun phrases and comment upon the effect created in the text.

- To be able to modify a noun to create an expanded noun phrase.

- To use expanded noun phrases to convey detailed information concisely.

Commentary

The three learning objectives ensure that children have a comprehensive understanding of an expanded noun phrase and its function within a sentence. It focuses children's attention on recognising this particular grammatical feature, knowing how it can be constructed and specifically refers to its purpose. Make sure that you explore these learning objectives with the children either prior to embarking upon the lesson or ask children to consider what the learning objectives might be once you have introduced the lesson. Asking the children to formulate the learning objective for themselves can often give you a valuable insight into their understanding of the lesson and encourages them to share in setting the expectations.

Starter: Information relay

Arrange the children into mixed-ability groups. You will also need an easel containing cards with various adjectives, determiners, prepositional phrases, nouns and verbs printed on them. These can be on different colours to distinguish the different word classes. Give each of the groups a noun which will act as the head word within the noun phrase. One child from each group takes it in turns to approach the easel and choose one of the cards to add to the noun. This can be done as a relay or a timed exercise. Alternatively, groups could use sticky notes to write various parts of a noun phrase according to your instructions or use pre-programmed tablets such as iPads to drag relevant parts of a sentence together.

This is an excellent starter for mixed-ability groups as all children will be working collaboratively to produce a sentence containing an expanded noun phrase.

Examples of words and phrases that could be included on the printed cards may include:

- nouns - cat, book, river, girls, cloud, trees;
- adjectives - sly, sad, old, interesting, beautiful;
- determiners - a, this, some, two, many, the;
- prepositional phrases - along the wall, in the ditch, on the table, in the sky, across the street, on the frozen path;
- verbs - crept, sang, slipped, swam, stand.

Groups could therefore choose words and phrases to make some of the following sentences:

> The sly cat crept along the wall.
>
> Some old trees stand in the forest.
>
> Two beautiful girls slipped on the frozen path.

At this point, children do not need to know that they are constructing sentences containing expanded noun phrases; they are just aware that they are expanding sentences to include more information. Once the relay has been completed the constituent parts of the sentence can be explored in more detail as appropriate for your class and the relevant terminology introduced or reinforced.

During this activity, identify those children who are unfamiliar with any of the grammatical features and how they can be used within a sentence. They may need some extra support during the independent activities in the form of prompts, writing frames or adult intervention.

Main lesson

Introduction

Choose an appropriate extract from a book that you have been reading with the children. For the purpose of this lesson example, I am going to refer to *The Secret Garden* by Frances Hodgson Burnett. Explain that we are going to produce our own poems based on this book and present them to parents during the class assembly later that term. You do not have to produce poetry; you could easily ask the children to write descriptive paragraphs based upon their own secret garden. Another alternative would be for children to write a diary extract from a character's point of view, describing that person's entrance into the garden.

> You have established a purpose for the writing by suggesting an audience for the children's written work (the visitors attending their assembly). Adapt your own lesson by using a book with which the children are familiar so that they can discuss how the author has used expanded noun phrases to add to the atmosphere and tone of the overall text. This will enable the children to gain a greater understanding of how to create similar effects in their own writing.

Choose an extract from the book which clearly demonstrates the use of expanded noun phrases, such as the first time Mary enters the secret garden. Read the extract together and ask the children to tell a partner what they now know about the secret garden. They can either list this on individual mini-whiteboards or a teaching assistant or yourself could act as a scribe and collate some of their ideas on the interactive whiteboard. Allow five to ten minutes for this discussion before asking the children to explain how they know this. Identify the words and phrases that provide detail and extra information, focusing upon the expanded noun phrases. Discuss these with children, identifying the main noun, the determiner, premodifiers and postmodifiers.

> Use talk partners or small discussion groups so that the children can share their thoughts and modify their answers based upon the opinions of others. According to Aidan Chambers, when we verbalise our thoughts to others, we are not simply clarifying them in our own mind:
>
> > The listener reflects on it and reflects it back to the speaker. Then we see what we've said 'in a different light'.
> >
> > (Chambers, 2011, p109)
>
> By asking the children to explain what they have learnt about the garden rather than asking them to highlight noun phrases, they are immediately

identifying the purpose of an expanded noun phrase and are much more likely to understand its function within the text.

Whether you use the terms premodifier and postmodifier or talk about words and phrases before and after the main noun is down to personal choice. However, the fact remains that children need to articulate their thoughts in such a way as to communicate meaning and you will need to be confident in your use of grammatical terminology if you use it within the classroom.

Examples of expanded noun phrases from our chosen text might include the following:

> The high walls which shut it in were covered with the leafless stems of climbing roses, which were so thick that they were matted together.

> The sun was shining inside the four walls and the high arch of sky over this particular piece of Misselthwaite seemed even more brilliant and soft than it was over the moor.

You may want to look at the phrases above and discuss how the author has provided further detail about the walls of the garden and the sky. In the first example, the main noun is 'walls'; the determiner is 'the'; the premodifier is the adjective 'high'. The postmodifier comprises all words appearing after the head and in this case is the finite clause which shut it in. More importantly, what effect do these sentences create within the body of the text? How do they convey the information? How do they add to the atmosphere of the scene?

Listen carefully to the children's answers and challenge their thinking with questions such as: Why do you think that? What makes you say that? Why do you disagree with your partner? Use this time to assess children's ability in identifying expanded noun phrases and explaining their function.

Following on from this lesson, you may want to take the children outside to a garden area within the school or visit a local park, arboretum or botanical garden if you have time. Whilst walking around the park or garden, encourage children to jot down words and phrases that come into their head or write them on large pieces of paper which can be displayed on the class working wall.

Critical questions to ask pupils include:

- What can you see, hear, smell, touch?

- How does it make you feel?

- How can you convey that feeling through your written words?

If you want your children to use description to provide a vivid picture within the minds of their reader, you need to allow them time to experience the very things that they are describing.

Practical application

Following a lesson in which you model writing a descriptive poem using expanded noun phrases, the children can compose their own poems based on either their recent visit to a park or using pictures of gardens as a stimulus. Encourage the children to create a strong mood or atmosphere and note the tone and impact of the description. To support and challenge the children in your class, you may wish to do the following:

- Provide writing frames for some children so that they can concentrate on inclusion of noun phrases rather than on poetic form.

- Guide or extend a group by working with them to improve sentence structure.

- Ask another adult to scribe for individuals or groups of children.

- Use a computer program such as Textease, My World or other bespoke primary software to create a vocabulary bank from which children can choose ideas and 'drag and drop' them into a writing frame.

> Depending upon your class and timetable, this lesson may be better taught as a series of lessons in which children could explore expanded noun phrases in more detail. They need to continue to develop their vocabulary and identify how the use of noun phrases can improve their writing.

Plenary

Ask the children to look at their poem and describe the mood using relevant adjectives. Can they highlight particularly effective noun phrases and explain the constituent parts? The children must now alter one or two of their sentences containing expanded noun phrases to suggest a different garden and change the atmosphere.

> By changing some of their sentences to suggest a withered and decaying garden rather than one in full bloom, they are consolidating their understanding of how the tone of their writing can be changed to reflect a different mood. This will help to enhance their writing, expand their vocabulary and demonstrate how they can manipulate texts to describe various scenes in a precise and concise manner.

Assessment (measuring achievement)

Assessment for learning

- Prior knowledge of your children's ability will enable you to plan work successfully at an appropriate yet challenging level. Take the time during the starter to listen to conversations, extend discussions and note any children who may be struggling with sentence structure.

- You may want to give each child a noun and ask them to modify it using different grammatical features, for example, add an adverb, add a prepositional phrase. This will provide useful information when embarking upon this lesson.

Assessment at the point of learning

- Work with a guided group to ascertain what they know about nouns and noun phrases. Use questions such as those included in the lesson plan to assess whether they have an understanding of how expanded noun phrases work.

- Ask children to identify expanded noun phrases during guided reading and discuss why the author has chosen to include specific information.

- Use mini-plenaries during the lesson to question children and ask them to explain what they have learnt to a partner or yourself.

Assessment of learning

When marking the children's work, you will need to refer to the learning objectives that you set at the beginning of the lesson and consider the following questions:

- Have pupils correctly identified expanded noun phrases?

- Are they using them effectively to communicate precise information?

- Have the pupils demonstrated accurate use of expanded noun phrases?

Challenges

- Children will need to have a secure knowledge of nouns, their function and how to use noun phrases within a sentence. Depending upon their stage of development, some children may start by adding an adjective before the main noun and progress to using alternative determiners, adverbs, verbs and clauses. Structure this progression appropriately.

- Expanded noun phrases tend to appear more frequently in books that may be appropriate for better readers. Some children may need simpler texts or more support during shared reading. You know the children in your class and provision should be made to ensure all children can access the learning.

- Expanded noun phrases can by their very nature grow into uncontrolled strings of descriptive phrases which are far too long and complex in structure. You may need to look at examples where this is the case and ask children to suggest why it is not as effective.

- With long strings of descriptive words and phrases, it is easy to write them down as they pop into your head. Make sure that your pupils understand that the order of these words and phrases is important. Would you write the *blue winding long river* or the *long blue winding river?* Oral rehearsal is important before committing ideas to paper.

Application of learning

Links to other areas of the curriculum

Noun phrases convey extra information about the noun in a very efficient way and prevent written texts from becoming too boring. They help to create a scene and set the mood of the writing. They dominate writing, accounting for the majority of the text, and are used extensively in narratives, personal recounts, biographies, historical reports and poetry. They can also feature quite strongly in scientific reports which communicate information to the reader about a particular subject. Although the example above is based on poetry, there are many opportunities to reinforce the use of expanded noun phrases. For example:

- Science: writing reports or factual accounts of scientific phenomena;

- History: reports based on eye-witness accounts describing a particular event;

- Geography: factual writing about geographical features;

- Art: representations of description.

Next lesson

When thinking about the next lesson, consider whether the children in your class are using noun phrases appropriately. If not, you may want to form a guided writing group to look specifically at the structure of an expanded noun phrase and explore their own writing to make improvements. To develop learning further, provide children with the opportunity to adapt their poem or narrative text to convey a different atmosphere. Use words to paint a very different picture from the one that they have previously written. Instead of a summer evening, can they write as though they were experiencing the garden on a cold December morning? Describe the trees, the pond and the children playing. How is this different from their first account?

Learning outcomes review

You should now have a greater understanding of the structure of an expanded noun phrase and its constituent parts. You are more familiar with the terminology and should feel confident to discuss this with your class. Through the lesson plan and commentary, you should have a developing understanding of how you can teach expanded noun phrases in the classroom and why children need to understand how they can enhance and improve their writing.

The lesson plan is intended as one way in which you can introduce your Year 5 class to expanded noun phrases and has been structured so as to allow you to adapt it for the needs of individuals and groups of individuals within your class. You can substitute *The Secret Garden* with a book with which you are more familiar so that you are able to choose the most suitable extracts to share during shared and guided reading. Use your professional judgement when applying aspects of the lesson plan to address the varying abilities within your own class.

Points to consider

- Differentiation: how could you address the needs of all pupils?
- Could you adapt this lesson to teach other grammatical features?
- Will you use correct terminology with the children when discussing grammatical features within a text?

Further reading

Department for Children, Schools and Families (DCSF) (2009) *Support for Spelling*. London: DCSF.

This is a useful document for subject knowledge and progression.

Department for Education (DfE) (2013) *The National Curriculum in England: Framework Document*. London: DfE.

The 2014 National Curriculum provides a comprehensive appendix setting out requirements for each year group. In addition, there is a very useful glossary which provides definitions for common grammatical terms.

Medwell, J., Moore, G., Wray, D. and Griffiths, V. (2012) *Primary English: Knowledge and Understanding*, 6th edn. London: Sage/Learning Matters.

The chapter entitled 'The grammar of the sentence in Standard English' explores the way in which sentences are structured and explains the component parts of the English sentence, clearly linking subject knowledge to classroom practice.

References

Burnett, F.H. (2012) *The Secret Garden*. London: Random House (first published 1911).

Chambers, A. (2011) *Tell Me: Children, Reading and Talk.* Stroud: Thimble Press.

Department for Education (DfE) (2013) *The National Curriculum in England: Framework Document*. London: DfE.

Morpurgo, M. (2000) *From Hereabouts Hill*. London: Egmont Books.

Morpurgo, M. (2000) *Kensuke's Kingdom*. Glasgow: Egmont Books.

Rowling, J.K. (1998–2009) *Harry Potter* series. London: Bloomsbury.

Chapter 11

Year 6: Using the subjunctive form in speech

Learning outcomes

Some aspects of grammar can seem difficult due to their limited application in English, despite having a clear function in other languages. The subjunctive form is one such aspect. It is one of the finite verb phrases or moods (along with the indicative and the imperative) and this chapter explores how this feature of language can be given purpose and meaning within formal public speaking.

This chapter will allow you to achieve the following outcomes:

- understand how the subjunctive form can be used in formal speech (and writing);
- understand how this type of verb phrase or mood expresses a wish, hope or intention.

Teacher's Standards

Working through this chapter will help you meet the following standards:

1. Set high expectations which inspire, motivate and challenge pupils.
2. Promote good progress and outcomes by pupils.
3. Demonstrate good subject and curriculum knowledge.
4. Plan and teach well-structured lessons.
6. Make accurate and productive use of assessment.

Links to the National Curriculum

Lower Key Stage 2 statutory requirement

Years 5 and 6

SPOKEN LANGUAGE (Years 1–6)

Pupils should be taught to:

- use relevant strategies to build their vocabulary;
- articulate and justify answers, arguments and opinions;
- speak audibly and fluently with an increasing command of Standard English;

- participate in discussions, presentations, performances, role play, improvisations and debates;
- gain, maintain and monitor the interest of the listener(s);
- select and use appropriate registers for effective communication.

WRITING

Vocabulary, grammar and punctuation

Pupils should be taught to:

- develop their understanding of the concepts set out in Appendix 2 by:

  ✓ recognising vocabulary and structures that are appropriate for formal speech and writing, including subjunctive forms
  ✓ using relative clauses beginning with who, which, where, when, whose, that or with an implied (i.e. omitted) relative pronoun.

(DfE, 2013)

Key focus: The subjunctive form

In 1965 *Fowler's Modern English Usage* stated:

> *About the subjunctive, so delimited, the important general facts are: (1) that it is moribund except in a few easily specified uses; (2) that, owing to the capricious influence of the much analysed classical moods upon the less studied native, it probably never would have been possible to draw up a satisfactory table of the English subjunctive uses; (3) that assuredly no one will ever find it either possible or worthwhile to do so now that the subjunctive is dying; and (4) that subjunctives met with today, outside the few truly living uses, are either deliberate revivals, especially by poets, for legitimate enough archaic effect, or antiquated survivals giving a pretentious flavour to their context, or new arrivals possible only in an age to which the grammar of the subjunctive is not natural but artificial.*

(Fowler, 1965, p595)

Why is it then that nearly 50 years later the subjunctive is still a feature of grammar teaching? It would seem that, despite Fowler, the subjunctive has clung on in formalised speech and writing; it is even highlighted in the revised National Curriculum for 2014 as a statutory part of what should be taught in maintained schools (referred to at the beginning of this chapter). The subjunctive mood is a feature of ancient languages, for example Latin, and more modern counterparts such as French, Italian and Spanish and is used in these languages to express uncertainty as opposed to facts. In English grammar, the subjunctive mood can be difficult to explain because of its hypothetical nature: it is a way of using verbs formally to express a wish, command or potential prospective event.

It is useful to note that, in terms of verbs and their usage, mood does not mean disposition or attitude. It actually refers to the mode or type of verb being used in any given context. In the case of the subjunctive, the verb form is finite, which means it is being used to indicate tense. If you have been taught a language other than English at school you have probably learned to conjugate verbs (and survived it!). In order to understand finite verb forms it is useful to have a go at conjugation, as it will demonstrate what happens to the verb in some contexts (depending on person and tense). For example, when conjugating the verb (*to*) *be* in the present tense we change it to reflect the person:

I am

You are (singular)

She/he is

We are

You are (plural)

They are

You will notice that some of the verb forms stay the same (when following you/we/they). Regular verbs have even fewer changes to remember.

Activity

Consider the way the following verbs look when conjugated in the present tense. If it is helpful, do this in a table like Table 11.1.

Table 11.1   Conjugating verbs

Verb: present tense	First person (singular)	Second person (singular)	Third person (singular)	First person (plural)	Second person (plural)	Third person (plural)
e.g. Eat	I eat	You eat	She/he/it eats	We eat	You eat	They eat
Drink						
Watch						
Swim						

It is only really in the third person singular that any change is noticeable: an 's' is added to the word (sometimes an 'es', as in *watches*). This means that the subjunctive form is only really noticeable in the third person singular as the verb reverts to the form used in first and second person. But what exactly is the subjunctive form? In simple terms, it is a verb phrase which shows *whether a clause is expressing a factual, non-factual, or directive meaning* (Crystal, 1988, p84). For example:

The medical evidence suggests that people <u>refrain</u> from smoking.

I <u>move</u> that the motion be carried.

The teachers insist we <u>follow</u> the school rules.

Her mother asks that she <u>walk</u> to the shops to buy milk.

The underlined words are the finite verbs which indicate the subjunctive form. You will notice that the third example includes an omitted or implied relative pronoun (*that*); also, the final sentence does not sound as natural as the other sentences.

Activity

- Think about the sentences given as examples of the subjunctive mood above. Why does the final sentence sound less fluent? When is it appropriate to use the subjunctive?
- Investigate the way the subjunctive mood or form is defined in foreign language teaching. Consider how these definitions might help you explain this element of sentence construction to your class.

How children learn about the subjunctive mood

In order to understand the concept of subjunctive forms children need to be able to draw upon an understanding of sentence structure, in particular the difference between clauses and phrases. Prior learning will have included an understanding of subordination and modal verbs; it should also have included a full range of grammatical terms to enable them to describe accurately the function of individual words in sentences. Children would need to know the infinitive forms of verbs and have an awareness of conjugation in order to hear the difference in the way the subjunctive form appears in the third person singular.

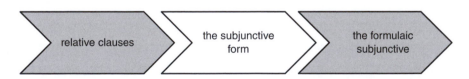

relative clauses → the subjunctive form → the formulaic subjunctive

Figure 11.1   Learning about the subjunctive mood

The subjunctive offers an alternative to conditional forms of verb phrases using should/could/might: it is a more formalised way of expressing hypothetical intentions or proposals. Learning about this type of sentence construction allows children to choose different registers for their writing and talk depending on the formality of the context, which is a requirement of the National Curriculum for 2014.

Teaching your class: Year 6

Year 6 is a time for consolidation, but it is also the beginning of transition to Key Stage 3. As part of the new programmes of study for 2014 pupils are expected to present themselves confidently and appropriately in a range of formalised situations (Figure 11.2).

Spoken English

Pupils should be taught to:

- speak confidently and effectively, including through:
  - using Standard English confidently in a range of formal and informal contexts, including classroom discussion
  - giving short speeches and presentations, expressing their own ideas and keeping to the point
  - participating in formal debates and structured discussions, summarising and/or building on what has been said

Figure 11.2   Extract from the National Curriculum (**https://www.gov.uk/government/uploads/system/ uploads/attachment_data/file/244215/SECONDARY_national_curriculum_-_English2.pdf**)

Learning techniques for formal writing and speaking at this stage, and being able to recognise their effect, will prepare them for the demands of the next key stage in their learning.

Context

The children in this Year 6 class have been learning about persuasive writing in different contexts: they know the key features of this kind of text. They are familiar with the word classes and have a command of metalanguage that enables them to analyse sentences. They have seen Standard English usage modelled, both in written and oral form, and they are familiar with a range of speaking and listening activities, including partner talk and group discussion.

Previous lessons have included a field trip to the local park and a survey of class viewpoints about the facilities available.

Learning objectives

- To use the subjunctive mood in a formal speech in order to:
  - emphasise your point;
  - express a hope or wish (aspiration) for the future.
- To compare different ways of making the same point in a persuasive text.

Commentary

Learning objectives identify what the pupils will be able to do as a result of the learning and can be linked to Bloom's taxonomy. This will enable you to be specific about the sort of activity needed to achieve the objective; it also helps you plan challenging tasks to stretch your learners.

Bloom's taxonomy is often represented in a pyramid form, with higher-level thinking skills coming at the pinnacle (Figure 11.3).

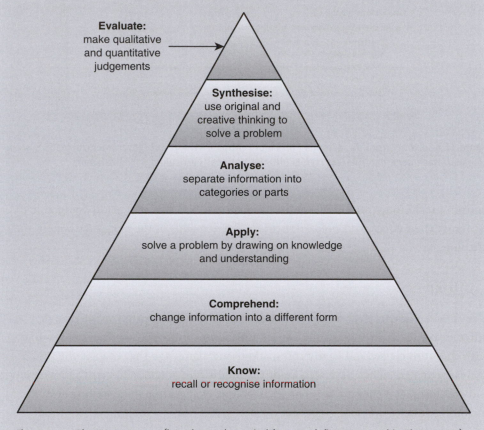

Evaluate:
make qualitative and quantitative judgements

Synthesise:
use original and creative thinking to solve a problem

Analyse:
separate information into categories or parts

Apply:
solve a problem by drawing on knowledge and understanding

Comprehend:
change information into a different form

Know:
recall or recognise information

Figure 11.3 Bloom's taxonomy (based on a theoretical framework first presented in Bloom, 1956)

Recently it has been reimagined and slightly reordered to reflect the place of creating within learning. As a pyramid, it somehow suggests a hierarchy, although it might be more useful to think of the arrangement of elements as a cycle. Sometimes we want to draw from different categories when planning, not because they are easier but because they are necessary at that point in the learner's development (Figure 11.4).

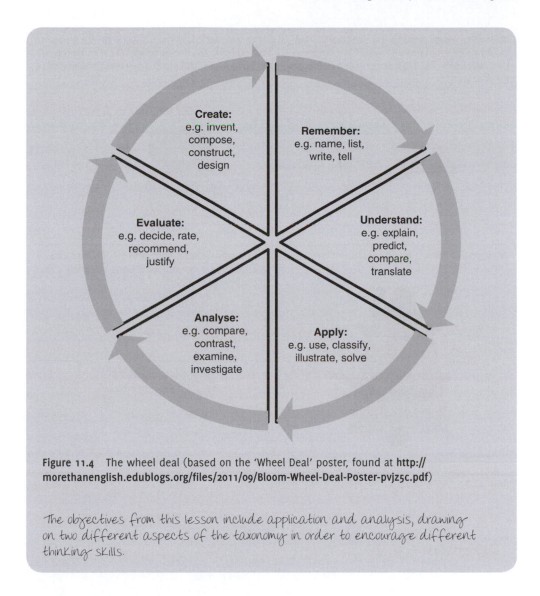

Figure 11.4 The wheel deal (based on the 'Wheel Deal' poster, found at **http:// morethanenglish.edublogs.org/files/2011/09/Bloom-Wheel-Deal-Poster-pvjz5c.pdf**)

The objectives from this lesson include application and analysis, drawing on two different aspects of the taxonomy in order to encourage different thinking skills.

Lesson opener: Talking posh

Explain that the first activity is all about practising 'posh talk', i.e. speaking using more formal words and phrases. Hand out talk cards to the pupils in pairs and allow them to choose which activity to do. If they have draft books or working journals encourage them to make notes; otherwise give them paper for collating/mind mapping ideas. Make sure you emphasise that it is the talk that is the focus of the activity, not the note taking.

Suggested talk cards are shown in Figure 11.5.

Give the pupils five minutes for the task and set an audible timer. Monitor the discussions, querying language and syntax choices where appropriate.

You invent a new word for the dictionary: what would it be? What does it mean? Is it a noun, verb, adjective, etc.? Come up with a definition for your word. 	Your telephone is ringing, but you do not recognise the number. You decide to answer it . . . it turns out to be Queen Elizabeth II! What does she say to you? Why has she called? 
What do you think is being said here? Why? 	You receive a letter from your local MP asking for your views on your local park. What will you include in your reply? 

Figure 11.5 Using more formal words and phrases

Commentary

All of the activities lend themselves to pupils using more formal Standard English in their speech. The dictionary activity allows the pupils to use other entries as models (as long as you make sure dictionaries are available and of an appropriate standard); the phone call from the Queen and the courtroom scene enable an element of role play; and the reply to the MP's letter allows those who feel confident speaking formally to use their own voice. It is important that you monitor the pupils' understanding of Standard English and intercede if you feel they are not using an appropriate vocabulary or language structure, for example verb tense agreement, avoiding contractions.

When the timer ends ask the pupils to reflect on how their language and vocabulary choice were affected by the scenario. On sticky notes get them to write one statement that explains what they have noticed about the way they spoke during the activity, encouraging them to use the metalanguage they are already familiar with, and then ask them to group their statements around labels on a display board entitled 'Vocabulary', 'Syntax' and 'Use of voice'.

Commentary

By encouraging the children to think about their intended audience from the examples above, you are getting them into the right mind set for learning about the subjunctive. This means they are not 'translating' from the informal speech they might have used with their friends prior to the lesson into more formal patterns, as they are already thinking in this way. The display will aid the main part of the lesson and encourages the children to reflect on their own learning, promoting good outcomes.

Main lesson

Introduction

Give out a sticky note per child. Allow one minute to come up with a point which can be included on a list of success criteria for persuasive texts. At the end of the minute ask them to group their success criteria in groups of four; if they have too many that are similar, ask them to check with other groups to see if they can swap sticky notes to create lists that cover the main features expected from this type of writing (alternatively they can write extra points out for their group). These will need to be displayed somewhere the whole group will be able to see: on the wall near their desks, or in the middle of a group of tables, for example.

Commentary

Pupils in Year 6 should be able to generate the generic success criteria for each of the non-fiction text types quite easily if they have been taught consistently. It is important that they establish those elements of the text type that are transferable, for example the use of superlatives, the use of the second person to engage the reader, the single point of view being argued or presented. By starting the lesson this way you are encouraging children actively to recall their prior learning rather than telling them what has been learned before.

Explain to the pupils that they are going to prepare a short persuasive speech. It will be written in a formal way as it will be used as the basis for a letter to the local council about the facilities the class would like to see at the local park. In order to make our persuasive talk sound formal we are going to add a new item to our list of success criteria: the use of the subjunctive form. Hand out prepared sticky notes to each group with this item on it so they can add it to their items.

The teacher then shows the class the following sentences, allowing two minutes to discuss (this time in pairs) which sounds more formal:

Build a ski ramp in the park.

Please build a ski ramp in the park.

We would like you to build a ski ramp in the park.

We request that you build a ski ramp.

The pupils should identify the last sentence as being the most formal and give their reasons.

Commentary

At this stage in the lesson it is useful to monitor the discussion and praise the appropriate use of metalanguage, for example if any of the children identify the first sentence as being in the imperative, or link it to instructions; if they identify the use of the modal auxiliary verb 'would' or comment on the use of 'request' as a verb and not a noun.

You then need to unpick how the last sentence works, annotating the key elements, as shown in Table 11.2.

Table 11.2 Deconstructing a formal sentence

We	request	that	you	build	a	ski	ramp
Noun (first person plural)	Verb	Conjunction	Noun (second person singular)	Verb (finite)	Determiner	Adjective	Noun
		Relative (subordinate) clause					

Explain how this sentence uses a relative clause to express an aspiration for the future – in this case, the hope that the council will build the suggested ski ramp. The use of a verb like 'request' *before* the relative clause indicates that this is not happening now, even though the sentence is in the present tense. Demonstrate how other key verbs can replace *request* but still make sense, for example *suggest* or *demand*: how do these words change the tone of the sentence? The sentence is still formal, but *demand* sounds more forceful and less open to negotiation.

Set the task of writing a short speech in pairs which rehearses the key points they want to use to persuade the council to make changes in the park, drawing upon their notes from the recent field trip and their surveys. Give the pupils the key questions shown in Figure 11.6 to act as prompts and encourage them to use the subjunctive in their speeches.

What do you demand?
What do you request?
What do you suggest?
What do you advise?
What do you insist?

Figure 11.6 Prompts for the subjunctive

The speeches can be written or recorded depending on the pupils' access to the necessary technology and their personal preference; whichever method is chosen, there must be a record of the key points of their argument to support the intended letter-writing task for which this is an oral rehearsal.

Commentary

Encourage the pupils to be highly selective rather than using all of the options listed above; for example, do they really feel demands are appropriate in this type of persuasion? For those who are confidently using the subjunctive, suggest they leave out the word 'that' in some of their sentences to avoid unnecessary repetition: where does omitting the word work best without affecting the meaning of the sentence?

It should be noted that this kind of oral rehearsal of a formal text allows pupils to hear the different registers, tones and language necessary to communicate in a range of situations and is good practice for any kind of writing that is different from their normal, day-to-day communication.

Plenary

The original groups of four should now work together in order to peer-assess the speeches. Each pair presents in turn, and feedback should reflect the agreed success criteria from the sticky notes generated at the start of the activity. You can then ask pairs to highlight elements of good practice in the others' speech that they feel have met the criteria for success.

Commentary

By encouraging the pupils to peer-assess they are not only benefitting from the feedback: they are hearing other members of the class modelling Standard English phrases in a formal way. This is only possible if you, as the teacher, have addressed misconceptions throughout the lesson, so ensure you scaffold the main task for those who may find this change of voice most difficult.

Assessment (measuring achievement)

Assessment for learning

- The paired work will enable you to hear aloud the use of language from individuals, so it is important that you address any grammatical errors or issues inappropriate for formal speaking and writing at this stage.

- The use of oral rehearsal should enable children to write more formally, but only if they have understood how formal Standard English sounds. Pupils who struggle to use a range of 'voices' can be given access to clips from formal speeches – the Queen's Christmas address, for example – to provide a model.

Assessment at the point of learning

- Look for children attempting to use words other than those suggested ('demand', 'suggest', etc.) to create their own sentences using the subjunctive, as this will demonstrate their ability and understanding.

Assessment of learning

This needs to be explicitly linked back to the lesson's learning objectives. Have the children achieved the following?

- To be able to use the subjunctive mood in formal speech.

- To select the most appropriate ways of making a point in a persuasive text, i.e. not overusing the subjunctive or using it inappropriately.

It would be helpful to use recordings of the pupils' speeches to enable them to assess their own learning at this point. They can reflect upon the coherence of their speech and their ability to use the subjunctive mood in a way that feels appropriate rather than interjected into their talk without a logical link to the subject being discussed.

Challenges

- Children will need to be able to use metalanguage to discuss verb forms and Standard English.

- Using the subjunctive mood in formal speech is possible even if you are not able to articulate what the subjunctive mood is, especially in the case of formulaic constructions. As a class teacher you need to decide when it is important for children to be able to explain the grammatical feature as well as utilise it in their writing.

Application of learning

Links to other areas of the curriculum

Because the subjunctive mood features in many of the languages pupils may have the opportunity to study at secondary school there is obviously a link between learning it now and applying this to foreign language learning. It can also be used across the curriculum in the following subjects:

- English: non-fiction text types such as discussion and persuasion often use formal Standard English, and subjunctive forms can help the text sound more official;

- Geography: the 'suggest/recommend' pattern can be used when writing about issues such as town planning and development;

- Art: when children are reflecting and peer-assessing they can use 'I suggest . . ./I advise . . .' statements to help them formulate appropriate guidance.

Next lesson

There are formulaic subjunctive forms which can be explored, for example:

Suffice it to say . . .

Far be it for me to . . .

Be that as it may . . .

The pupils can research the meaning of the key words and devise their own 'rules' for when such phrases might be useful.

There is also the *were-subjunctive* or *past subjunctive* (Crystal, 1988, p85) which uses *if . . . were* to express meaning, for example, 'If we were on holiday . . .'; 'If she were here . . .'. Again, pupils can explore the way this expression can be used and when it would be appropriate to do so.

Learning outcomes review

You should now understand how the subjunctive form can be used in formal speech (and writing) and how this type of verb phrase or mood expresses a wish, hope or intention. You should be able to recognise how the finite form of the verb can be used to indicate an unreal or non-factual situation. You should feel confident in guiding pupils through reflective discussions about appropriate registers for effective communication using suitable terminology and metalanguage.

Points to consider

- How important do you think it is that children can recognise this sentence construction as the subjunctive? Consider the impact on future language learning if we avoid the technical terminology at this stage.

Further reading

Waugh, D. and Jolliffe, W. (2013) *English 5–11: A Guide for Teachers*. London: David Fulton.

Although this book does not include definitions for more complex grammatical terms, it does have a very useful chapter on 'Knowledge about language: grammar and punctuation'. The chapter contains advice and strategies for planning effective grammar lessons.

References

Bloom, B.S. (1956) *Taxonomy of Educational Objectives: The Classification of Educational Goals, by a Committee of College and University Examiners. Handbook I: Cognitive Domain*. New York: Longmans, Green.

Crystal, D. (1988) *Rediscover Grammar*. Harlow: Longman.

Department for Education (DfE) (2013) *The National Curriculum in England: Framework Document*. London: DfE.

Fowler, H.W. (1965) *Fowler's Modern English Usage*, 2nd edn. London: Oxford University Press.

Chapter 12

Year 6: Using the passive voice

Learning outcomes

Sentences are units of grammatical meaning which, at the very least, contain subjects (noun phrases) and predicates (containing the verb). However, in some sentences the subject is implied rather than made explicit, with the logical object becoming the subject: we describe these sentences as being in the passive voice as opposed to the active voice. This chapter explores the way sentences can be constructed in the passive voice and addresses the purpose for using this particular sentence construction.

This chapter will allow you to achieve the following outcomes:

- develop an understanding of the active and passive voice;
- have an awareness of the ways different sentence structures can be used for effect;
- consider engaging ways in which sentence structures can be taught.

Teachers' Standards

Working through this chapter will help you meet the following standards:

2. Promote good progress and outcomes by pupils.
3. Demonstrate good subject and curriculum knowledge.
4. Plan and teach well-structured lessons.
6. Make accurate and productive use of assessment.

Links to the National Curriculum

Lower Key Stage 2 statutory requirement

Years 5 and 6

READING

Comprehension

Pupils should be taught to:

- understand what they read by:
  - ✓ identifying how language, structure and presentation contribute to meaning
- discuss and evaluate how authors use language, including figurative language, considering the impact on the reader

WRITING

Composition

Pupils should be taught to:

- draft and write by:
  - ✓ selecting appropriate grammar and vocabulary, understanding how such choices can change and enhance meaning

Vocabulary, grammar and punctuation

Pupils should be taught to:

- develop their understanding of the concepts set out in Appendix 2 by:
  - ✓ using passive verbs to affect the presentation of information in a sentence.

(DfE, 2013)

Key focus: The active and passive voice

The way we structure sentences affects the importance we place on certain elements. Writers can emphasise the subject/agent, the action or even the object by using different voices; they can make a sentence sound more formal or impersonal, allowing the writer to distance him- or herself from what is being written. For example, compare the following:

> Suzanne and Branwen have written this book to help teachers in the classroom teach grammar.

> This book has been written in order to help teachers in the classroom teach grammar.

Although the sentences provide very similar information, they differ in structure, effect and emphasis. In the first the agent is clear: the subjects have been identified (*Suzanne* and *Branwen*) and their actions are explicit. However, the tone or voice sounds inappropriate for this kind of handbook; also, as the authors are clearly identified on the front cover there is no need to repeat their agency continually throughout the text. In other words, a more impersonal or passive voice is required.

In order to turn an active sentence into a passive one the changes shown in Figure 12.1 take place.

The passive voice is usually constructed by combining the verb *be* with a past participle, although you can also use *get* with the past participle to create passive sentences. Passive sentences using *get* do not generally contain an agent: it is more likely you will hear *I got pushed over* (*get* plus past participle) or *I was pushed over by the large dog* (*be* plus past participle) than *I got pushed over by the large dog*. This is a convention rather than a rule, with passive sentences containing *be* used in formal English and *get* used in informal.

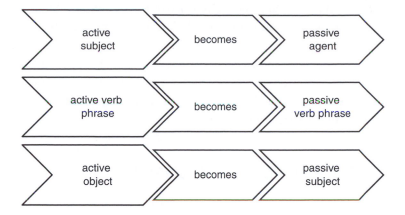

Figure 12.1 Changing to passive

Crystal (1996, p118) models the transformation of an active sentence to a passive one as shown in Figure 12.2.

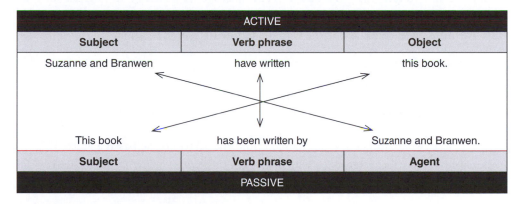

Figure 12.2 Transforming active to passive

Activity

Underline the active sentences and circle the passive sentences below. Try changing the voice from active to passive or passive to active.

- The children broke the window.
- The dogs barked at the postman.
- The painting was stolen.
- The events during the trial were watched with interest.
- The teacher enjoyed teaching grammar.

What extra information is required to change some sentences from passive to active?

Not all sentences can be changed from the active voice to the passive, and some of the sentences that can be changed sound forced or lack fluency. Think about the last example in the activity above: if grammar is the active object, does the sentence make sense when it becomes the passive subject? And which verb should become the focus of the passive verb phrase: enjoyed or teaching? For example, should the sentence be *Grammar was taught with enjoyment by the teacher* or *Grammar was enjoyed by the teacher when taught?* Neither sounds particularly convincing.

How children learn about the passive voice

In order to use the passive voice in their speech and writing, children need to understand verbs and verb phrases. However, the main difficulty in understanding how to use the passive voice comes from not knowing the difference between transitive and intransitive verbs. Intransitive verbs have no object and thus cannot be changed from active to passive. A transitive verb can take an object, and in some cases has to be linked to an object in order to make sense. Some verbs can be transitive or intransitive; some are always transitive; and others can only be intransitive. As a teacher you will need to be able to recognise when a verb is intransitive, as it will be impossible for the pupils to make active sentences into passive ones in these cases. In order to understand fully the difference, think about the way the following sentences sound:

> The children waited. (Intransitive)
> The dog barked. (Intransitive)
> Did you enjoy the film? (Transitive)
> I found the TV remote. (Transitive)

Only the last two examples can be changed from the active to the passive voice: it is impossible to construct a sentence which changes *the children* or *the dog* into passive agents because there is no object in the sentence to become the passive subject.

Children will have explored the perfect tense in Year 3 (see Chapter 6) and modal verbs in Year 5 (see Chapter 9) so should already be familiar with the use of auxiliary verbs to support main verbs.

Sometimes there is confusion between the passive and the present perfect. As the guidance on the British Council's website states, *Confusion can occur because 'have been' can be the (active voice) present perfect form of 'be'* **and** *it can be part of a passive form (present perfect passive).* Misconceptions can also arise around the use of the *be* plus *past participle* construction in

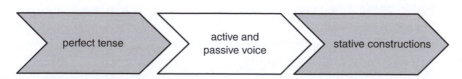

Figure 12.3 Learning about the passive voice

stative and dynamic sentences: stative describes a state of affairs (*My car was broken beyond repair*) and dynamic, sometimes called *eventive*, describes action (*My car was broken into by thieves*). Only the dynamic example is in the passive voice, even though they both contain *was broken* as a verb phrase. These are all discussions children will need to have if they are really to understand what a passive sentence is.

Teaching your class: Year 6

By Year 6 children should be comfortable text-marking and analysing language use; they should also have a considerable grasp of the metalanguage necessary to support that analysis, although key terms that have only recently been introduced may need to be displayed with definitions as reminders. This lesson is not intended to cover all aspects of the learning necessary to understand fully how to construct sentences in the passive voice, and it should be understood that this is a concept that needs to be returned to in different contexts.

Context

As part of a sequence of lessons on journalistic recount the children have already analysed the layout of a range of newspapers. They know the difference between broadsheets, tabloids and local newspapers and have analysed the use of a range of literary features, such as chronological recount; the use of who/when/what/where/why and how in the opening paragraph; and the use of the third person. The pupils enjoy a class novel, and have shared the first chapter of *Percy Jackson and the Lightning Thief* by Rick Riordan.

Learning objectives

- To use passive verbs to affect the presentation of information.
- To compose an impersonal text using Standard English.

Commentary

The lesson is focused on the composition of texts rather than the analysis, so even though some analysis might happen as part of the activities, it is not an objective for learning. Try to avoid putting all aspects of learning you want the children to apply from previous lessons as objectives, as this will take the focus off new learning.

Lesson opener: Whodunit?

Put the children into pairs and hand out packs of flashcards with illustrations of key characters from fairy stories or well-known tales, for example Peter Pan, Cinderella,

Jack, Red Riding Hood, The Little Mermaid and Aladdin. Using presentational software (for example, PowerPoint) show the children a description of events and explain they have to hold up the correct character linked to the events.

Commentary

The activity establishes the link between the characters as subjects and events or actions specific to them. It does rely on a shared cultural understanding of the texts being referred to, so you will need to be aware of any English as additional language learners or children who have a different cultural, social or ethnic history. It is relatively easy to include stories from different home cultures if you take the time to research different folklores and traditional tales from other countries.

Show the children a predicate like . . . *climbed a beanstalk to steal the golden goose.* Children should hold up the picture of Jack. Do a quick-fire series of predicates, with more than one for each character shown in a random sequence, for one minute.

Commentary

Sentences are quite difficult to explain, even though everyone uses the concept when using language. The usual definitions talk about groups of words that make sense, but this doesn't offer any kind of explanation as to why one group of words makes sense when another doesn't. In order to address this, some grammar texts define sentences as always having a subject and a predicate; sometimes they also include an object.

In simple terms, the subject and object refer to nouns or noun phrases (who), while the predicate details the verb phrase and other information pertaining to events (what/when/how/why).

Then tell the children you are going to do the same thing again, but this time it may not be as clear who the predicate refers to, for example . . . *is male* (could be Aladdin, could be Jack). They have to try and group all the possible responses each time. Try to be as inventive as possible for this one!

Commentary

This activity is introducing the idea that the subject is not always obvious, and that sometimes we can have events described for which more than one person is potentially responsible. The statements you write need to be based on your choice of texts due to the reasons mentioned above regarding pupils' cultural capital, and will require you to know something about the texts you have selected.

The children should start to see that sometimes more than one answer is possible, and that it is not always possible to identify the subject because we are not sure who the sentence was written about: we can only take a best guess based on the possible options.

Main lesson

Introduction

Collect in the cards and give the pairs a copy of a local news article which contains explicit examples of the passive voice, such as the one shown in Figure 12.4.

Man arrested after Greek statue stolen from museum

© School Paper Press 2014   Monday 1st January 2014

A man has been arrested after a statue was stolen from the National Museum late last night.

Police were called to reports of a possible theft after the absence of the statue was noticed by security guards patrolling the museum.

Police have been puzzled by the disappearance of the statue

A police spokesperson said, "The statue is a priceless artefact which the museum is keen to recover. A man has been taken into custody and officers would like to speak to anyone who thinks they may have information in connection with this incident."

Figure 12.4   Newspaper article

Display the following question: Who arrested the man? Allow one minute for talking partners to come up with a response. The most likely answer is *the police* but this is not explicitly stated: why not? Explain this sentence is written in the passive voice rather than the active voice, and that you will explain a bit more about the passive voice after the next activity.

Ask the children to devise a series of *Who* questions based on the article. They should identify the following examples linked to passive sentences:

Who stole the statue?

Who called the police?

Who noticed the statue was missing?

Commentary

This lesson follows the REDM sequence for teaching grammar put forward by Reedy and Bearne (2013, p7) which encourages the teaching of grammar in context (Figure 12.5).

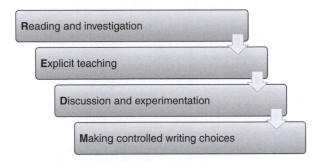

Figure 12.5 REDM sequence for teaching grammar

The initial reading and investigation allow pupils to explore language in use, allowing them to see the link between audience, purpose and effect. As the class teacher, you will need to be secure in your own subject knowledge in order to support this investigation, in the same way you would make sure you were aware of possible outcomes to a science experiment before providing the opportunity to investigate chemical reactions!

Discuss the different reasons why the subject or agent of the action/event might be hidden or omitted. Some of the sentences are written about obvious agents: the police, security guards, etc. Some are written about an unknown agent, for example, the person who phoned the police.

Commentary

This discussion is very important to establish the idea that we can still write about an event even if we don't know who is responsible. Often passive voice is taught by changing active sentences into passive ones, but this lesson is about using the passive voice from the start because it serves a particular purpose, i.e. it is formal, impersonal and it allows the writer to omit the agent where appropriate.

Pick out one of the sentences for deconstruction. The first sentence is a useful one in the article above because it is a compound sentence providing two examples of the passive voice in use. Using a visualiser or whiteboard, do a shared analysis of the grammatical features, asking the children to pick out what they felt made the sentence passive as opposed to active.

Commentary

The children should be able to identify aspects like the following (Figure 12.6).

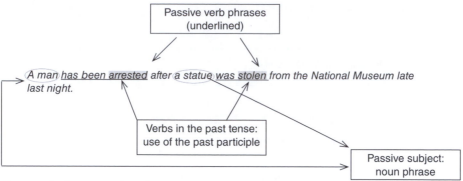

Figure 12.6 Deconstruction of a sentence

At this stage it may be helpful to share one of the models used earlier in this chapter in order to help the children understand how the sentence has been structured, such as the one provided by David Crystal (1996) (Figure 12.7).

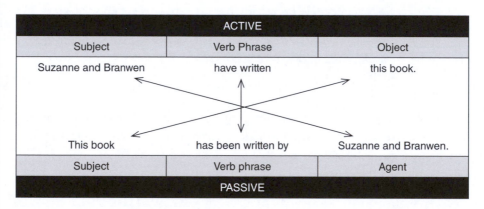

Figure 12.7 Transforming active to passive

Then give the pupils two minutes to look at the other sentences within the text to pick out the passive objects and verb phrases. What happens if they try to make any of the sentences active? How does it change the tone and formality of the text?

Commentary

This will enable you to make clear the link between 'be' and the past participle: the use of the word 'has' in the first sentence is a red herring and does not always feature in passive sentences, whereas there is always a conjugation, or variation of the form, of the verb 'be' (am/are/is/was/were/been).

Practical application

Give out the following activity card based on the events from the relevant chapter of the class novel, in this case Chapter 1 of *Percy Jackson and the Lightning Thief*, and explain that the children are going to write their own local news article about a mysterious event in the museum.

Reporter's Notebook

Possible headline: Mysterious Dust Found in Museum

Key witnesses:

- Security guard – found the dust
- Cleaner – had to try and remove it from exhibits
- School Party? Did they see anything?

Facts:

_____
_____
_____
_____

Figure 12.8 Activity card

The children, acting as journalists, can return to the text to gather information useful to their article. They must remember that only Percy seems to know how the dust appeared: Percy's class teacher was vaporised (by Percy!) and disappeared in a cloud of yellow powder which smelled of sulphur. However, as journalists, do they think they would believe this story when the rest of the class can't even remember that the teacher existed?

Once they feel they have enough information they can start writing their article, using the passive voice to imitate the impersonal style of the news article from the introduction.

Plenary

Pupil as teacher

During the writing activity, select a class member or pair who appear to be confidently using the passive voice, particularly pupils who are not relying on the verb *have* as part of the sentence construction. Tell them they are going to take over as the teacher at the end of the independent task by briefly summarising what they learned about this particular way of constructing a text and questioning the other class members to see what they know.

Commentary

By enabling children who are confidently applying the learning to explain to the class you are allowing them to take a responsible attitude to their own learning (part of the Teachers' Standards) but you are also able to see if they really are aware of how the passive voice is constructed or if they were copying a pattern with no intellectual engagement.

Give all the pupils a sticky note and ask them to identify something about constructing texts they did not know at the beginning of the lesson but now feel they understand/can do. Collect in for assessment.

Assessment (measuring achievement)

Assessment for learning

- The children need to have a grasp of the metalanguage for text-marking grammatical features, so you will need to explore their ability to use terms like subject, noun and object in the starter activity.

- They will also need to be secure in the key features of journalistic recount.

The purpose of this lesson is not to learn how to write a newspaper article; it is to apply the conventions of newspaper writing and introduce the concept of passive voice with omitted or implied agent. With this in mind, it is important you as the teacher remember to focus on the new learning.

Assessment at the point of learning

- Ensure that anyone supporting the children within the lesson is aware of the link between the verb *be* and the past participle, and that they understand transitive verbs, as these are the key areas to look out for in the children's writing.

- Any children who you feel may struggle with writing in the passive voice should be given the opportunity to work in a guided group during the newspaper activity. This will enable you to address misconceptions at the point of need.

Assessment of learning

The plenary sticky note activity will enable you to see what the pupils think they have learned; this can then be attached to their article when marking for you to comment on.

When marking the article, you will need to consider the following questions:

- Have the pupils demonstrated their ability to construct sentences in the passive voice?

- Have the pupils understood that the important elements of the verb phrase are *be* + *past participle*?

- Have any of the pupils tried to use intransitive verbs or construct sentences that do not read fluently? This will then need to be addressed through guided reading and writing.

Challenges

- Most of the challenges, such as the need to recognise when a verb or verb phrase is transitive, have been discussed earlier in this chapter. However, one of the key things to remember is that it is how you address this over time, in a range of contexts, that will impact most on the children's learning.

- Using the correct subject vocabulary when analysing grammatical features should be actively encouraged in Year 6.

- The confusion caused by similar sentence constructions, for example, the past perfect, may need to be unpicked in order to address misconceptions that prevent confident and accurate use of the passive voice.

Application of learning

Links to other areas of the curriculum

Passive tense is most frequently used in writing of an impersonal nature. It is commonly found in write-ups of scientific investigations where it is not necessary to know who did the task, for example, *The plant needed regular watering.* Using the active voice when writing means the subject has to be identified, and this can cause complications when hypothesising: what if the member of the group chosen to be responsible for watering the plant is not available? The important thing is that the action happens, not who does it. The passive tense can also be used to write explanations, recounts and reports when a formal, impersonal voice is required. For example:

- Science: written records of experiments, processes and observations;

- History: formal recounts of events, such as: *In 1066 the Battle of Hastings was won by the army of William the Conqueror;*

- Design and Technology: when investigating and analysing a range of existing products, the passive voice allows the pupils to write about a product's features without knowing who made it (but only if the past participle is used, as use of the present participle makes the sentence construction stative not passive).

Next lesson

It is worth asking the pupils to identify other genres and text types that they feel will benefit from the use of a passive voice. A display can be set up to remind them of this grammar feature and the areas they identify. In their final year of Key Stage 2 they should be starting to see how these features can be applied rather than viewing them as discrete and disconnected sentence types.

Learning outcomes review

This chapter has explored an aspect of grammar teaching that is deceptively simple and often done through providing a model for imitation rather than an explicit underpinning of how and why the passive voice is used. The REDM approach to teaching grammar in context, explained by Reedy and Bearne (2013), provides an excellent way of planning for meaningful learning but relies totally on teachers' subject knowledge. Without this, you will be unable to identify the key features of the passive voice or choose appropriate examples from texts. In order to help children discuss and evaluate how authors use language, or how to select appropriate grammar and use passive verbs to affect the presentation of information, you must first understand these things yourself.

Points to consider

- How can you secure your subject knowledge as part of the planning process?
- How many reference texts about the topic do you use regularly?
- Do you model learning about grammar to your pupils, or avoid problematic questions where possible?
- How can investigation and exploration of language in use support your learners in becoming effective writers?

Further reading

The British Council has a LearnEnglish site for children: **http://learnenglishkids.britishcouncil.org/en/**. Although active/passive voice is not discussed here (it does feature explicitly in the adult section of LearnEnglish), there are grammar exercises and games which will help consolidate pupils' understanding of the grammatical features needed to prepare for learning about the passive voice.

References

Crystal, D. (1996) *Discover Grammar*. Harlow: Longman.

Department for Education (DfE) (2013) *The National Curriculum in England: Framework Document*. London: DfE.

Reedy, D. and Bearne, E. (2013) *Teaching Grammar Effectively in Primary Schools*. UKLA.

Riordan, R. (2013) *Percy Jackson and the Lightning Thief*. London: Penguin Books.

Chapter 13

Moving on

Learning outcomes

This chapter will allow you to achieve the following outcomes:

- understand the importance of the learning environment when teaching grammar;
- understand how to adapt the lesson examples in previous chapters to suit the needs of your learners;
- develop strategies to inspire and support the writing process.

Teachers' Standards

Working through this chapter will help you meet the following standards:

3. Demonstrate good subject and curriculum knowledge.
4. Plan and teach well-structured lessons.
5. Adapt teaching to respond to the strengths and needs of all pupils.

Introduction

The lesson examples included in this book have all been tried and tested in the classroom and have successfully contributed to children's knowledge and understanding of grammatical concepts. A key feature of these lesson examples is that they build upon children's prior knowledge and their interests. They are not intended to be seen as a 'quick fix' to meet the requirements of English in the National Curriculum. Knowledge about grammar usage should lead to greater understanding of how we can manipulate words and sentences to create particular effects that will touch the heart of the reader. The intention is not to produce a generation of grammar pedants who apply rules and dissect texts in such a way as to destroy its very essence. By teaching grammar within meaningful contexts your lessons will motivate, engage and inspire your pupils to use grammar not only accurately but also creatively to produce writing that is fluid, cohesive and purposeful.

Adapting lesson examples

We have provided a great deal of background information so that you are able to situate the learning within a contextual framework; however, our ideas and examples can be easily adapted to suit the needs of your learners. The pedagogies associated with the teaching of grammar remain consistent but the suggested games and activities used to consolidate and apply learning are easily transferable. Whilst reading, you may have identified ways in which you can adapt the lessons to teach other aspects of grammar or changed the focus of the learning objective to reflect the demands of your classroom best. In the same way that we expect children to use grammar creatively to address their purpose, we would anticipate that you use the guidance contained in this book to address your purpose.

Activity

Consider one of the examples from Chapters 3–12 and make notes on how you could use the framework provided to teach an element of grammar pertinent to your year group.

- How have you adapted the lesson?
- Which elements can be consistently applied to your lesson?
- What subject knowledge do you need to have in order to teach the concept effectively?

These questions are crucial when using the guidance contained within the book to plan lessons that address the particular learning needs and styles of your pupils.

Creating the learning environment

An integral part of your classroom practice will be creating an environment that is conducive to learning. How do you ensure that your classroom supports the teaching of grammar with a purpose?

Physical environment

Working walls can be used to support and scaffold learning, acting as visual prompts and reminders for children when embarking upon writing activities. If you are introducing a new concept or building upon prior learning, use the working wall to display correct terminology and definitions as well as including examples of what this looks like in practice. For example, if your grammar focus is adverbials, your working wall may look like the example shown in Figure 13.1.

You may also want to display examples of texts with adverbial phrases highlighted and ask children to write on sticky notes why they think it is effective. This will reinforce how adverbials are used to create effect and allow the children to comment upon its suitability for the purpose. You could initiate discussion by asking why the author chose to tell the reader where something was taking place or how the choice of adverbial gives the reader a clear picture of how the characters are behaving. Furthermore, you could consider displaying examples from books that you have read in guided or shared reading sessions which clearly illustrate the purpose of adverbial phrases.

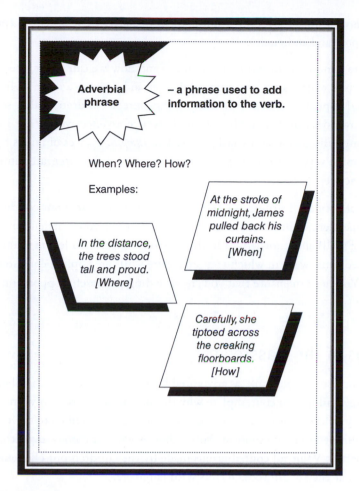

Figure 13.1   Working wall

A language-rich curriculum

The way in which you celebrate language in your classroom will send out messages as to how children can use it effectively in their own work. When discussing best practice for the teaching of early reading using systematic synthetic phonics, Rose argues strongly that this is

> *embedded within a broad and language-rich curriculum: that is to say, a curriculum that generates purposeful discussion, interest, application, enjoyment and high achievement across all the areas of learning and experience . . .*

> (Rose, 2006, p16)

The same can be said of the teaching of grammar. Discussion features significantly when talking about the author's choice of words and sentences: as children become more confident in articulating their opinions, they will be more likely to modify their word choices in light of such discussions. Asking children why they have included certain words or sentence structures allows them to clarify their decisions and relate them to purpose and audience.

If children are genuinely interested in language and how we can use it, they are able to take risks when using grammatical devices and develop a more stylistic and individualised approach in their own writing. Encourage children to alter sentence structure. How does this change the meaning? Is it more effective? Why? Ignite their interest through discussion and word games. The *Jumpstart* series of books by Pie Corbett has some very useful games and activities that can be integrated into your classroom practice.

Application of previous learning is essential if you are to prepare your children to become independent, confident and creative learners. Does your curriculum support application of skills and knowledge? In the previous chapters on lesson examples, we have addressed some ways in which you can ensure skills are applied consistently in other areas. You need to ensure that you are providing purposeful opportunities for this to take place.

The ethos of the classroom

Promoting the use of 'book talk' as advocated by Aidan Chambers (Chambers, 1985) will encourage children to contemplate why the author has chosen to write in a particular way. If the children in your class are confident to articulate their views, they are better equipped to make those authorial choices when it comes to putting pen to paper themselves. Value all contributions made by the children but challenge their thinking so that they begin to take risks with language.

Activity

The following two pieces of work have been written by the same pupil. The first is the original opening paragraph in which the child described a race between a cheetah and a monkey; the second is a redrafted version following input during a guided writing session focusing on the use of expanded noun phrases to aid description.

Reflect upon the two examples. Consider which paragraph is more effective and why. How do you think the teacher has encouraged the pupil to take risks? Identify the particular grammatical features that have been included in the second piece of work.

One lovely day in the jungle there was a yellow and black cheetah who kept boasting that he was the fastest creature. Then one day he started teasing a big, angry monkey because he was such a slow, lazy creature. Then the monkey said that if they had a race he would win. The cheetah was furious and shouted loudly at the monkey. They decided to race across the green swampy jungle until they reached the blue calm river.

The sun shone brightly in the jungle where the black spotted cheetah was boasting that he was the fastest creature in the whole of the jungle. One day he started teasing the biggest monkey in the forest because he was such a slow and lazy creature. The monkey argued that if they had a race he would win. The cheetah, who was furious, shouted loudly at the monkey. Immediately, each creature decided to race through the green swamps of the jungle until they reached the calm blue river.

Resources

Carefully evaluate the resources you use to teach your grammar lessons. There are many interactive whiteboard games that will engage children but how can you ensure that all children are actively engaged in the learning? Beware of games that allow only one child at a time to answer questions because there will be many more children left without a reason to contribute their ideas. The use of mini-whiteboards, sticky notes, talk partners and tablets will ensure that each child adds something to the discussion and will provide opportunities for you to make formative assessments.

Use reminders and prompts to encourage children to think about how they can include certain grammatical elements in their writing but steer away from lengthy checklists that require children to include ' four adjectives, a time connective, an ellipsis, a subordinate clause', etc. It is much more important that you demonstrate how the inclusion of particular features adds to the overall effect of the text rather than 'training' children to include particular techniques. This can be achieved through informed discussion and effective modelling where you are acting as the expert writer.

Conclusion

The requirements of the National Curriculum for 2014 dictate, to a certain extent, what has to be taught but it is your role to ensure that this is done in an engaging, stimulating and purposeful manner. One of the overarching aims of the Language and Literacy curriculum is that children are able to *write clearly, accurately and coherently, adapting their language and style in and for a range of contexts, purposes and audiences* (DfE, 2013, p13). By contextualising the teaching of grammar, you will avoid the boredom that will more than likely ensue if children are simply required to complete endless exercises to correct 'bad' grammar. If children can see how the use of grammatical conventions can enhance a piece of written work, they will be able to employ these in their own writing whilst considering the purpose and audience. Grammar can be used to increase creativity within the writing process rather than stifle the imagination if you, and the children you teach, value it as a repertoire of informed choices for expressing meaning through language.

Points to consider

- There is a strong case for teaching grammar at the point of use. How will you ensure that you are providing suitable opportunities to address this?

- Does your classroom support creativity within writing? Develop strategies to motivate and inspire writers, building upon existing learning and prior learning.

- How can you ensure that all children in your class are prepared to complete the statutory assessments in Year 6 whilst ensuring that grammar is used within a purposeful context? Are these notions mutually exclusive or is there a case for addressing both?

Learning outcomes review

You should now be aware of ways in which you can support the teaching of grammar within your classroom, using the learning environment to good effect. You should be able to consider how the ideas and commentaries included within the previous chapters can be adapted to teach grammar relevant to the needs of the children in your class. In exploring the subject-specific pedagogies, you will be able to use them regardless of the year group and ability of the children you teach, applying the underlying principles to your own teaching. You will also be aware of some of the strategies you might use to support and enthuse writers in your class, whether through discussion or the use of creative resources.

Further reading

Chambers, A. (2011) *Tell Me: Children, Reading and Talk.* Stroud: Thimble Press.

Together with his website, **www.aidanchambers.co.uk/index.htm**, this book offers an excellent insight into how discussion and talk help develop 'book talk' in the classroom which can in turn promote informative discussions that allow children to think about how the author has created atmosphere and effect.

Corbett, P. (2004) *Jumpstart Literacy.* Oxon: David Fulton Publishers.

This little book is packed with games and activities that can be used during Literacy lessons to encourage children to play with words and language.

Crystal, D. (2005) *How Language Works.* London: Penguin.

This is a fascinating book which provides comprehensive examples to enhance your own subject knowledge.

Waugh, D., Warner, C. and Waugh, R. (2013) *Teaching Grammar, Punctuation and Spelling in Primary Schools.* London: Sage.

This book explores subject knowledge for teachers and provides some excellent examples of classroom practice to illustrate how grammar can be taught in the primary classroom.

References

Chambers, A. (1985) *Booktalk*. London: Bodley Head.

Corbett, P. (2004) *Jumpstart Literacy*. Oxon: David Fulton Publishers.

Department for Education (DfE) (2013) *The National Curriculum in England: Framework Document*. London: DfE.

Rose, J. (2006) *Independent Review of the Teaching of Early Reading*. London: DfES.

Chapter 14

Glossary of terms

The following glossary of terms is taken directly from the National Curriculum for 2014 (DfE, 2013, p80). It should be intended as a point of reference, not a list of terms that children need to be taught. Definitions are for terminology found in the National Curriculum for 2014 and will help to clarify vocabulary used within this book.

Whilst exploring effective grammar lessons, we have referred to a number of books which will also be useful when clarifying terms and definitions so do not think of this as an exhaustive list of grammatical terminology; use alongside other books which develop subject knowledge.

Term	Guidance	Example
active voice	An active verb has its usual pattern of subject and object (in contrast with the passive).	Active: *The school arranged a visit.* Passive: *A visit was arranged* by the school.
adjective	The surest way to identify adjectives is by the ways they can be used: before a noun, to make the noun's meaning more specific (i.e. to modify the noun), or after the verb *be*, as its complement. Adjectives cannot be modified by other adjectives. This distinguishes them from nouns, which can be. Adjectives are sometimes called 'describing words' because they pick out single characteristics such as size or colour. This is often true, but it doesn't help to distinguish adjectives from other word classes, because verbs, nouns and adverbs can do the same thing.	*The pupils did some really good work.* [adjective used before a noun, to modify it] *Their work was good.* [adjective used after the verb *be*, as its complement] Not adjectives: *The lamp glowed.* [verb] *It was such a bright red!* [noun] *He spoke loudly.* [adverb] *It was a French grammar book.* [noun]
adverb	The surest way to identify adverbs is by the ways they can be used: they can modify a verb, an adjective, another adverb or even a whole clause. Adverbs are sometimes said to describe manner or time. This is often true, but it doesn't help to distinguish adverbs from other word classes that can be used as adverbials, such as preposition phrases, noun phrases and subordinate clauses.	*Usha soon started snoring loudly.* [adverbs modifying the verbs *started* and *snoring*] *That match was really exciting!* [adverb modifying the adjective *exciting*] *We don't get to play games very often.* [adverb modifying the other adverb, *often*] *Fortunately, it didn't rain.* [adverb modifying the whole clause *it didn't rain* by commenting on it]

Term	Guidance	Example
		Not adverbs: *Usha went up the stairs.* [preposition phrase used as adverbial] *She finished her work this evening.* [noun phrase used as adverbial] *She finished when the teacher got cross.* [subordinate clause used as adverbial]
adverbial	An adverbial is a word or phrase that is used, like an adverb, to modify a verb or clause. Of course, adverbs can be used as adverbials, but many other types of words and phrases can be used this way, including preposition phrases and subordinate clauses.	The bus *leaves in five minutes.* [preposition phrase as adverbial: modifies *leaves*] *She promised to see him last night.* [noun phrase modifying either *promised* or *see*, according to the intended meaning] *She worked until she had finished.* [subordinate clause as adverbial]
antonym	Two words are antonyms if their meanings are opposites.	*hot – cold* *light – dark* *light – heavy*
apostrophe	Apostrophes have two completely different uses: showing the place of missing letters (e.g. *I'm* for *I am*) marking possessives (e.g. *Hannah's mother*).	*I'm going out and I won't be long.* [showing missing letters] *Hannah's mother went to town in Justin's car.* [marking possessives]
article	The articles *the* (definite) and *a* or *an* (indefinite) are the most common type of determiner.	*The dog found a bone in an old box.*
auxiliary verb	The auxiliary verbs are: *be, have, do* and the modal verbs. They can be used to make questions and negative statements. In addition: *be* is used in the progressive and passive *have* is used in the perfect *do* is used to form questions and negative statements if no other auxiliary verb is present.	*They are winning the match.* [*be* used in the progressive] *Have you finished your picture?* [*have* used to make a question, and the perfect] *No, I don't know him.* [*do* used to make a negative; no other auxiliary is present] *Will you come with me or not?* [modal verb *will* used to make a question about the other person's willingness]
clause	A clause is a special type of phrase whose head is a verb. Clauses can sometimes be complete sentences. Clauses may be main or subordinate. Traditionally, a clause had to have a finite verb, but most modern grammarians also recognise non-finite clauses.	*It was raining.* [single-clause sentence] *It was raining but we were indoors.* [two finite clauses] *If you are coming to the party, please let us know.* [finite subordinate clause inside a finite main clause] *Usha went upstairs to play on her computer.* [non-finite clause]
cohesion	A text has cohesion if it is clear how the meanings of its parts fit together. Cohesive devices can help to do this. In the example, there are repeated references to the same thing (shown by the different style pairings) and the logical relations, such as time and cause, between different parts are clear.	**A visit** has been arranged for *Year 6*, to the Mountain Peaks Field Study Centre, leaving school at 9.30am. **This is an overnight visit.** The centre has beautiful grounds and *a nature trail.* During the afternoon, *the children* will follow *the trail.*

(Continued)

(Continued)

Term	Guidance	Example
cohesive device	Cohesive devices are words used to show how the different parts of a text fit together. In other words, they create cohesion. Some examples of cohesive devices are: determiners and pronouns, which can refer back to earlier words conjunctions and adverbs, which can make relations between words clear ellipsis of expected words.	*Julia's dad bought her a football. The football was expensive!* [determiner; refers us back to a particular football] *Joe was given a bike for Christmas. He liked it very much.* [the pronouns refer back to Joe and the bike] *We'll be going shopping before we go to the park.* [conjunction; makes a relationship of time clear] *I'm afraid we're going to have to wait for the next train. Meanwhile, we could have a cup of tea.* [adverb; refers back to the time of waiting] *Where are you going? [_] To school!* [ellipsis of the expected words *I'm going*; links the answer back to the question]
complement	A verb's subject complement adds more information about its subject, and its object complement does the same for its object. Unlike the verb's object, its complement may be an adjective. The verb *be* normally has a complement.	*She is our teacher.* [adds more information about the subject, *she*] *They seem very competent.* [adds more information about the subject, *they*] *Learning makes me happy.* [adds more information about the object, *me*]
compound, compounding	A compound word contains at least two root words in its morphology; e.g. *whiteboard, superman*. Compounding is very important in English.	*blackbird, blow-dry, bookshop, ice-cream, English teacher, inkjet, one-eyed, bone-dry, baby-sit, daydream, outgrow*
conjunction	A conjunction links two words or phrases together. There are two main types of conjunctions: co-ordinating conjunctions (e.g. *and*) link two words or phrases together as an equal pair subordinating conjunctions (e.g. *when*) introduce a subordinate clause.	*James bought a bat and ball.* [links the words *bat* and *ball* as an equal pair] *Kylie is young but she can kick the ball hard.* [links two clauses as an equal pair] *Everyone watches when Kyle does back-flips.* [introduces a subordinate clause] *Joe can't practise kicking because he's injured.* [introduces a subordinate clause]
consonant	A sound which is produced when the speaker closes off or obstructs the flow of air through the vocal tract, usually using lips, tongue or teeth. Most of the letters of the alphabet represent consonants. Only the letters *a, e, i, o, u* and *y* can represent vowel sounds.	/p/ [flow of air stopped by the lips, then released] /t/ [flow of air stopped by the tongue touching the roof of the mouth, then released] /f/ [flow of air obstructed by the bottom lip touching the top teeth] /s/ [flow of air obstructed by the tip of the tongue touching the gum line]
continuous	See progressive	
co-ordinate, co-ordination	Words or phrases are co-ordinated if they are linked as an equal pair by a co-ordinating conjunction (i.e. *and, but, or*). In the examples on the right, the co-ordinated elements are shown in bold, and the conjunction is underlined.	**Susan** <u>and</u> **Amra** met in a café. [links the words *Susan* and *Amra* as an equal pair] **They talked** <u>and</u> **drank tea** for an hour. [links two clauses as an equal pair] **Susan got a bus** <u>but</u> **Amra walked**. [links two clauses as an equal pair]

Term	Guidance	Example
	The difference between co-ordination and subordination is that, in subordination, the two linked elements are not equal.	Not co-ordination: *They ate before they met.* [*before* introduces a subordinate clause]
determiner	A determiner specifies a noun as known or unknown, and it goes before any modifiers (e.g. adjectives or other nouns). Some examples of determiners are: articles (*the*, *a* or *an*) demonstratives (e.g. *this*, *those*) possessives (e.g. *my*, *your*) quantifiers (e.g. *some*, *every*).	*the home team* [article, specifies the team as known] *a good team* [article, specifies the team as unknown] *that pupil* [demonstrative, known] *Julia's parents* [possessive, known] *some big boys* [quantifier, unknown] Contrast: *home the team*, *big some boys* [both incorrect, because the determiner should come before other modifiers]
digraph	A type of grapheme where two letters represent one phoneme. Sometimes, these two letters are not next to one another; this is called a split digraph.	The digraph *ea* in *each* is pronounced /iː/. The digraph *sh* in *shed* is pronounced /ʃ/. The split digraph *i–e* in *line* is pronounced /aɪ/.
ellipsis	Ellipsis is the omission of a word or phrase which is expected and predictable.	*Frankie waved to Ivana and she watched her drive away.* *She did it because she wanted to do it.*
etymology	A word's etymology is its history: its origins in earlier forms of English or other languages, and how its form and meaning have changed. Many words in English have come from Greek, Latin or French.	The word *school* was borrowed from a Greek word σχολή (*skholé*) meaning 'leisure'. The word *verb* comes from Latin *verbum*, meaning 'word'. The word *mutton* comes from French *mouton*, meaning 'sheep'.
finite verb	Every sentence typically has at least one verb which is either past or present tense. Such verbs are called 'finite'. The imperative verb in a command is also finite. Verbs that are not finite, such as participles or infinitives, cannot stand on their own: they are linked to another verb in the sentence.	*Lizzie does the dishes every day.* [present tense] *Even Hana did the dishes yesterday.* [past tense] *Do the dishes, Naser!* [imperative] Not finite verbs: *I have done them.* [combined with the finite verb *have*] *I will do them.* [combined with the finite verb *will*] *I want to do them!* [combined with the finite verb *want*]
fronting, fronted	A word or phrase that normally comes after the verb may be moved before the verb: when this happens, we say it has been 'fronted'. For example, a fronted adverbial is an adverbial which has been moved before the verb. When writing fronted phrases, we often follow them with a comma.	*Before we begin, make sure you've got a pencil.* [Without fronting: *Make sure you've got a pencil before we begin.*] *The day after tomorrow, I'm visiting my granddad.* [Without fronting: *I'm visiting my granddad the day after tomorrow.*]

(Continued)

(Continued)

Term	Guidance	Example
future	Reference to future time can be marked in a number of different ways in English. All these ways involve the use of a present-tense verb. See also tense. Unlike many other languages (such as French, Spanish or Italian), English has no distinct 'future tense' form of the verb comparable with its present and past tenses.	*He will leave tomorrow.* [present-tense *will* followed by infinitive *leave*] *He may leave tomorrow.* [present-tense *may* followed by infinitive *leave*] *He leaves tomorrow.* [present-tense *leaves*] *He is going to leave tomorrow.* [present tense *is* followed by *going to* plus the infinitive *leave*]
GPC	See grapheme–phoneme correspondences.	
grapheme	A letter, or combination of letters, that corresponds to a single phoneme within a word.	The grapheme *t* in the words *ten*, *bet* and *ate* corresponds to the phoneme /t/. The grapheme *ph* in the word *dolphin* corresponds to the phoneme /f/.
grapheme–phoneme correspondences	The links between letters, or combinations of letters (graphemes) and the speech sounds (phonemes) that they represent. In the English writing system, graphemes may correspond to different phonemes in different words.	The grapheme *s* corresponds to the phoneme /s/ in the word *see*, but . . . . . . it corresponds to the phoneme /z/ in the word *easy*.
head	See phrase.	
homonym	Two different words are homonyms if they both look exactly the same when written, and sound exactly the same when pronounced.	*Has he left yet? Yes – he went through the door on the left.* *The noise a dog makes is called a bark. Trees have bark.*
homophone	Two different words are homophones if they sound exactly the same when pronounced.	*hear, here* *some, sum*
infinitive	A verb's infinitive is the basic form used as the head-word in a dictionary (e.g. *walk, be*). Infinitives are often used: after *to* after modal verbs.	*I want to walk.* *I will be quiet.*
inflection	When we add *-ed* to *walk*, or change *mouse* to *mice*, this change of morphology produces an inflection ('bending') of the basic word which has special grammar (e.g. past tense or plural). In contrast, adding *-er* to *walk* produces a completely different word, *walker*, which is part of the same word family. Inflection is sometimes thought of as merely a change of ending, but, in fact, some words change completely when inflected.	*dogs* is an inflection of *dog*. *went* is an inflection of *go*. *better* is an inflection of *good*.
intransitive verb	A verb which does not need an object in a sentence to complete its meaning is described as intransitive. See transitive verb.	*We all laughed.* *We would like to stay longer, but we must leave.*

Term	Guidance	Example
main clause	A sentence contains at least one clause which is not a subordinate clause; such a clause is a main clause. A main clause may contain any number of subordinate clauses.	*It was raining but the sun was shining.* [two main clauses] *The man **who wrote it** told me **that it was true**.* [one main clause containing two subordinate clauses] *She said, 'It rained all day.'* [one main clause containing another]
modal verb	Modal verbs are used to change the meaning of other verbs. They can express meanings such as certainty, ability or obligation. The main modal verbs are *will, would, can, could, may, might, shall, should, must* and *ought*. A modal verb only has finite forms and has no suffixes (e.g. *I sing – he sings*, but not *I must – he musts*).	*I can do this maths work by myself.* *This ride may be too scary for you!* *You should help your little brother.* *Is it going to rain? Yes, it might.* *Canning swim is important.* [not possible because *can* must be finite; contrast: *Being able to swim is important*, where *being* is not a modal verb]
modify, modifier	One word or phrase modifies another by making its meaning more specific. Because the two words make a phrase, the modifier is normally close to the modified word.	In the phrase *primary-school teacher*: *teacher* is modified by *primary-school* (to mean a specific kind of teacher) *school* is modified by *primary* (to mean a specific kind of school).
morphology	A word's morphology is its internal make-up in terms of root words and suffixes or prefixes, as well as other kinds of change such as the change of *mouse* to *mice*. Morphology may be used to produce different inflections of the same word (e.g. *boy – boys*), or entirely new words (e.g. *boy – boyish*) belonging to the same word family. A word that contains two or more root words is a compound (e.g. *news+paper, ice+cream*).	*dogs* has the morphological make-up: *dog + s*. *unhelpfulness* has the morphological make-up: *unhelpful + ness* where *unhelpful = un + helpful* and *helpful = help + ful*
noun	The surest way to identify nouns is by the ways they can be used after determiners such as *the*: for example, most nouns will fit into the frame 'The __ matters/matter.' Nouns are sometimes called 'naming words' because they name people, places and 'things'; this is often true, but it doesn't help to distinguish nouns from other word classes. For example, prepositions can name places and verbs can name 'things' such as actions. Nouns may be classified as **common** (e.g. *boy, day*) or **proper** (e.g. *Ivan, Wednesday*), and also as **countable** (e.g. *thing, boy*) or **non-countable** (e.g. *stuff, money*). These classes can be recognised by the determiners they combine with.	*Our dog bit the burglar on his behind!* *My big brother did an amazing jump on his skateboard.* *Actions speak louder than words.* Not nouns: *He's behind you!* [this names a place, but is a preposition, not a noun] *She can jump so high!* [this names an action, but is a verb, not a noun] common, countable: *a book, books, two chocolates, one day, fewer ideas* common, non-countable: *money, some chocolate, less imagination* proper, countable: *Marilyn, London, Wednesday*

(Continued)

(Continued)

Term	Guidance	Example
noun phrase	A noun phrase is a phrase with a noun as its head, e.g. *some foxes, foxes with bushy tails*. Some grammarians recognise one-word phrases, so that *foxes are multiplying* would contain the noun *foxes* acting as the head of the noun phrase *foxes*.	*Adult foxes can jump.* [*adult* modifies *foxes*, so *adult* belongs to the noun phrase] *Almost all healthy adult foxes in this area can jump.* [all the other words help to modify *foxes*, so they all belong to the noun phrase]
object	An object is normally a noun, pronoun or noun phrase that comes straight after the verb and shows what the verb is acting upon. Objects can be turned into the subject of a passive verb, and cannot be adjectives (contrast with complements).	*Year 2 designed puppets.* [noun acting as object] *I like that.* [pronoun acting as object] *Some people suggested a pretty display.* [noun phrase acting as object] Contrast: *A display was suggested.* [object of active verb becomes the subject of the passive verb] *Year 2 designed pretty.* [incorrect, because adjectives cannot be objects]
participle	Verbs in English have two participles, called 'present participle' (e.g. *walking, taking*) and 'past participle' (e.g. *walked, taken*). Unfortunately, these terms can be confusing to learners, because: they don't necessarily have anything to do with present or past time although past participles are used as perfects (e.g. *has eaten*) they are also used as passives (e.g. *was eaten*).	*He is walking to school.* [present participle in a progressive] *He has taken the bus to school.* [past participle in a perfect] *The photo was taken in the rain.* [past participle in a passive]
passive	The sentence *It was eaten by our dog* is the passive of *Our dog ate it*. A passive is recognisable from: the past participle form *eaten* the normal object (*it*) turned into the subject the normal subject (*our dog*) turned into an optional preposition phrase with *by* as its head the verb *be* (*was*), or some other verb such as *get*. Contrast active. A verb is not 'passive' just because it has a passive meaning: it must be the passive version of an active verb.	*A visit was arranged by the school.* *Our cat got run over by a bus.* Active versions: *The school arranged a visit.* *A bus ran over our cat.* Not passive: *He received a warning.* [past tense, active *received*] *We had an accident.* [past tense, active *had*]
past tense	Verbs in the past tense are commonly used to: talk about the past talk about imagined situations make a request sound more polite.	*Tom and Chris showed me their new TV.* [names an event in the past] *Antonio went on holiday to Brazil.* [names an event in the past; irregular past of *go*] *I wish I had a puppy.* [names an imagined situation, not a situation in the past]

Term	Guidance	Example
	Most verbs take a suffix -ed, to form their past tense, but many commonly used verbs are irregular. See also tense.	*I was hoping you'd help tomorrow.* [makes an implied request sound more polite]
perfect	The perfect form of a verb generally calls attention to the consequences of a prior event; for example, *he has gone to lunch* implies that he is still away, in contrast with *he went to lunch*. 'Had gone to lunch' takes a past time point (i.e. when we arrived) as its reference point and is another way of establishing time relations in a text. The perfect tense is formed by: turning the verb into its past participle inflection adding a form of the verb *have* before it. It can also be combined with the progressive (e.g. *he has been going*).	*She has downloaded some songs.* [present perfect; now she has some songs] *I had eaten lunch when you came.* [past perfect; I wasn't hungry when you came]
phoneme	A phoneme is the smallest unit of sound that signals a distinct, contrasting meaning. For example: /t/ contrasts with /k/ to signal the difference between *tap* and *cap* /t/ contrasts with /l/ to signal the difference between *bought* and *ball*. It is this contrast in meaning that tells us there are two distinct phonemes at work. There are around 44 phonemes in English; the exact number depends on regional accents. A single phoneme may be represented in writing by one, two, three or four letters constituting a single grapheme.	The word *cat* has three letters and three phonemes: c/a/t The word *catch* has five letters and three phonemes: c/a/tch The word *caught* has six letters and three phonemes: c/augh/t
phrase	A phrase is a group of words that are grammatically connected so that they stay together, and that expand a single word, called the 'head'. The phrase is a noun phrase if its head is a noun, a preposition phrase if its head is a preposition, and so on; but if the head is a verb, the phrase is called a clause. Phrases can be made up of other phrases.	*She waved to her mother.* [a noun phrase, with the noun *mother* as its head] *She waved to her mother.* [a preposition phrase, with the preposition *to* as its head] *She waved to her mother.* [a clause, with the verb *waved* as its head]
plural	A plural noun normally has a suffix -s or -es and means 'more than one'. There are a few nouns with different morphology in the plural (e.g. *mice*, *formulae*).	*dogs* [more than one dog]; *boxes* [more than one box] *mice* [more than one mouse]
possessive	A possessive can be: a noun followed by an apostrophe, with or without -s a possessive pronoun.	*Tariq's book* [Tariq has the book] *The boys' arrival* [the boys arrive] *His obituary* [the obituary is about him] *That essay is mine.* [I wrote the essay]

(Continued)

(Continued)

Term	Guidance	Example
	The relation expressed by a possessive goes well beyond ordinary ideas of 'possession'. A possessive may act as a determiner.	
prefix	A prefix is added at the beginning of a word in order to turn it into another word. Contrast suffix.	*overtake, disappear*
preposition	A preposition links a following noun, pronoun or noun phrase to some other word in the sentence. Prepositions often describe locations or directions, but can describe other things, such as relations of time. Words like *before* or *since* can act as either prepositions or as conjunctions.	*Tom waved goodbye to Christy. She'll be back from Australia in two weeks.* *I haven't seen my dog since this morning.* Contrast: *I'm going, since no one wants me here!* [conjunction: links two clauses]
preposition phrase	A preposition phrase has a preposition as its head followed by a noun, pronoun or noun phrase.	*He was in bed.* *I met them after the party.*
present tense	Verbs in the present tense are commonly used to: talk about the present talk about the future. They may take a suffix -s (depending on the subject). See also tense.	*Jamal goes to the pool every day.* [describes a habit that exists now] *He can swim.* [describes a state that is true now] *The bus arrives at three.* [scheduled now] *My friends are coming to play.* [describes a plan in progress now]
progressive	The progressive (also known as the 'continuous') form of a verb generally describes events in progress. It is formed by combining the verb's present participle (e.g. *singing*) with a form of the verb *be* (e.g. *he was singing*). The progressive can also be combined with the perfect (e.g. *he has been singing*).	*Michael is singing in the store room.* [present progressive] *Amanda was making a patchwork quilt.* [past progressive] *Usha had been practising for an hour when I called.* [past perfect progressive]
pronoun	Pronouns are normally used like nouns, except that: they are grammatically more specialised it is harder to modify them In the examples, each sentence is written twice: once with nouns, and once with pronouns (underlined). Where the same thing is being talked about, the words are shown in bold.	**Amanda** waved to **Michael**. **She** waved to **him**. **John's** mother is over there. **His** mother is over there. The **visit** will be an overnight **visit**. **This** will be an overnight **visit**. **Simon** is the person: **Simon** broke it. **He** is the one **who** broke it.
punctuation	Punctuation includes any conventional features of writing other than spelling and general layout: the standard punctuation marks . , ; : ? ! - – ( ) " " ' ' , and also word spaces, capital letters, apostrophes, paragraph breaks and bullet points. One important role of punctuation is to indicate sentence boundaries.	*'I'm going out, Usha, and I won't be long,'* *Mum said.*

Term	Guidance	Example
Received Pronunciation	Received Pronunciation (often abbreviated to RP) is an accent which is used only by a small minority of English speakers in England. It is not associated with any one region. Because of its regional neutrality, it is the accent which is generally shown in dictionaries in the UK (but not, of course, in the USA). RP has no special status in the National Curriculum.	
register	Classroom lessons, football commentaries and novels use different registers of the same language, recognised by differences of vocabulary and grammar. Registers are 'varieties' of a language which are each tied to a range of uses, in contrast with dialects, which are tied to groups of users.	*I regret to inform you that Mr Joseph Smith has passed away.* [formal letter] *Have you heard that Joe has died?* [casual speech] *Joe falls down and dies, centre stage.* [stage direction]
relative clause	A relative clause is a special type of subordinate clause that modifies a noun. It often does this by using a relative pronoun such as *who* or *that* to refer back to that noun, though the relative pronoun *that* is often omitted. A relative clause may also be attached to a clause. In that case, the pronoun refers back to the whole clause, rather than referring back to a noun. In the examples, the relative clauses are underlined, and both the pronouns and the words they refer back to are in bold.	*That's the **boy** <u>who lives near school</u>.* [*who* refers back to *boy*] *The **prize** <u>**that** I won</u> was a book.* [*that* refers back to *prize*] *The **prize** <u>I won</u> was a book.* [the pronoun *that* is omitted] ***Tom broke the game***, <u>**which** annoyed Ali</u>. [*which* refers back to the whole clause]
root word	Morphology breaks words down into root words, which can stand alone, and suffixes or prefixes which can't. For example, *help* is the root word for other words in its word family such as *helpful* and *helpless*, and also for its inflections such as *helping*. Compound words (e.g. *help-desk*) contain two or more root words. When looking in a dictionary, we sometimes have to look for the root word (or words) of the word we are interested in.	*played* [the root word is *play*] *unfair* [the root word is *fair*] *football* [the root words are *foot* and *ball*]
schwa	The name of a vowel sound that is found only in unstressed positions in English. It is the most common vowel sound in English. It is written as /ə/ in the International Phonetic Alphabet. In the English writing system, it can be written in many different ways.	
sentence	A sentence is a group of words which are grammatically connected to each other but not to any words outside the sentence.	*John went to his friend's house. He stayed there till tea-time.*

(Continued)

(Continued)

Term	Guidance	Example
	The form of a sentence's main clause shows whether it is being used as a statement, a question, a command or an exclamation. A sentence may consist of a single clause or it may contain several clauses held together by subordination or co-ordination. Classifying sentences as 'simple', 'complex' or 'compound' can be confusing, because a 'simple' sentence may be complicated, and a 'complex' one may be straightforward. The terms **single-clause sentence** and **multi-clause sentence** may be more helpful.	*John went to his friend's house, he stayed there till tea-time.* [This is a 'comma splice', a common error in which a comma is used where either a full stop or a semi-colon is needed to indicate the lack of any grammatical connection between the two clauses.] *You are my friend.* [statement] *Are you my friend?* [question] *Be my friend!* [command] *What a good friend you are!* [exclamation] *Ali went home on his bike to his goldfish and his current library book about pets.* [single-clause sentence] *She went shopping but took back everything she had bought because she didn't like any of it.* [multi-clause sentence]
split digraph	See digraph.	
Standard English	Standard English can be recognised by the use of a very small range of forms, such as *those books, I did it* and *I wasn't doing anything* (rather than their non-Standard equivalents); it is not limited to any particular accent. It is the variety of English which is used, with only minor variation, as a major world language. Some people use Standard English all the time, in all situations from the most casual to the most formal, so it covers most registers. The aim of the National Curriculum is that everyone should be able to use Standard English as needed in writing and in relatively formal speaking.	*I did it because they were not willing to undertake any more work on those houses.* [formal Standard English] *I did it cos they wouldn't do any more work on those houses.* [casual Standard English] *I done it cos they wouldn't do no more work on them houses.* [casual non-Standard English]
stress	A syllable is stressed if it is pronounced more forcefully than the syllables next to it. The other syllables are unstressed.	*ab<u>out</u>* *<u>vi</u>sit*
subject	The subject of a verb is normally the noun, noun phrase or pronoun that names the 'do-er' or 'be-er'. The subject's normal position is: just before the verb in a statement just after the auxiliary verb in a question. Unlike the verb's object and complement, the subject can determine the form of the verb (e.g. *I am, you are*).	*Rula's mother went out.* *That is uncertain.* *The children will study the animals.* *Will the children study the animals?*
subjunctive	In some languages, the inflections of a verb include a large range of special forms which are used typically in subordinate clauses, and are called 'subjunctives'. English has very few such forms and those it has tend to be used in rather formal styles.	*The school requires that all pupils be honest.* *The school rules demand that pupils not enter the gym at lunchtime.* *If Zoë were the class president, things would be much better.*

Term	Guidance	Example
subordinate, subordination	A subordinate word or phrase tells us more about the meaning of the word it is subordinate to. Subordination can be thought of as an unequal relationship between a subordinate word and a main word. For example: an adjective is subordinate to the noun it modifies subjects and objects are subordinate to their verbs. Subordination is much more common than the equal relationship of co-ordination. See also subordinate clause.	*big dogs* [*big* is subordinate to *dogs*] *Big dogs need long walks.* [*big dogs* and *long walks* are subordinate to *need*] *We can watch TV when we've finished.* [*when we've finished* is subordinate to *watch*]
subordinate clause	A clause which is subordinate to some other part of the same sentence is a subordinate clause; for example, in *The apple that I ate was sour*, the clause *that I ate* is subordinate to *apple* (which it modifies). Subordinate clauses contrast with co-ordinate clauses, as in *It was sour but looked very tasty*. (Contrast: main clause) However, clauses that are directly quoted as direct speech are not subordinate clauses.	*That's the street where Ben lives.* [relative clause; modifies *street*] *He watched her as she disappeared.* [adverbial; modifies *watched*] *What you said was very nice.* [acts as subject of *was*] *She noticed an hour had passed.* [acts as object of *noticed*] Not subordinate: *He shouted, 'Look out!'*
suffix	A suffix is an 'ending', used at the end of one word to turn it into another word. Unlike root words, suffixes cannot stand on their own as a complete word. Contrast prefix.	*call – called* *teach – teacher* [turns a verb into a noun] *terror – terrorise* [turns a noun into a verb] *green – greenish* [leaves word class unchanged]
syllable	A syllable sounds like a beat in a word. Syllables consist of at least one vowel, and possibly one or more consonants.	*Cat* has one syllable. *Fairy* has two syllables. *Hippopotamus* has five syllables.
synonym	Two words are synonyms if they have the same meaning, or similar meanings. Contrast antonym.	*talk – speak* *old – elderly*
tense	In English, tense is the choice between present and past verbs, which is special because it is signalled by inflections and normally indicates differences of time. In contrast, languages like French, Spanish and Italian have three or more distinct tense forms, including a future tense. (See also future.) The simple tenses (present and past) may be combined in English with the perfect and progressive.	*He studies.* [present tense – present time] *He studied yesterday.* [past tense – past time] *He studies tomorrow, or else!* [present tense – future time] *He may study tomorrow.* [present tense + infinitive – future time] *He plans to study tomorrow.* [present tense + infinitive – future time] *If he studied tomorrow, he'd see the difference!* [past tense – imagined future] Contrast three distinct tense forms in Spanish: *Estudia.* [present tense] *Estudió.* [past tense] *Estudiará.* [future tense]

(Continued)

(Continued)

Term	Guidance	Example
transitive verb	A transitive verb takes at least one object in a sentence to complete its meaning, in contrast to an intransitive verb, which does not.	*He loves Juliet.* *She understands English grammar.*
trigraph	A type of grapheme where three letters represent one phoneme.	*High, pure, patch, hedge*
unstressed	See stress.	
verb	The surest way to identify verbs is by the ways they can be used: they can usually have a tense, either present or past (see also future). Verbs are sometimes called 'doing words' because many verbs name an action that someone does; while this can be a way of recognising verbs, it doesn't distinguish verbs from nouns (which can also name actions). Moreover many verbs name states or feelings rather than actions. Verbs can be classified in various ways: for example, as auxiliary, or modal; as transitive or intransitive; and as states or events.	*He lives in Birmingham.* [present tense] *The teacher wrote a song for the class.* [past tense] *He likes chocolate.* [present tense; not an action] *He knew my father.* [past tense; not an action] Not verbs: *The walk to Halina's house will take an hour.* [noun] *All that surfing makes Morwenna so sleepy!* [noun]
vowel	A vowel is a speech sound which is produced without any closure or obstruction of the vocal tract. Vowels can form syllables by themselves, or they may combine with consonants. In the English writing system, the letters *a, e, i, o, u* and *y* can represent vowels.	
word	A word is a unit of grammar: it can be selected and moved around relatively independently, but cannot easily be split. In punctuation, words are normally separated by word spaces. Sometimes, a sequence that appears grammatically to be two words is collapsed into a single written word, indicated with a hyphen or apostrophe (e.g. *well-built, he's*).	*headteacher* or *head teacher* [can be written with or without a space] *I'm going out.* *9.30 am*
word class	Every word belongs to a word class which summarises the ways in which it can be used in grammar. The major word classes for English are: noun, verb, adjective, adverb, preposition, determiner, pronoun, conjunction. Word classes are sometimes called 'parts of speech'.	
word family	The words in a word family are normally related to each other by a combination of morphology, grammar and meaning.	*teach – teacher* *extend – extent – extensive* *grammar – grammatical – grammarian*

Reference

Department for Education (DfE) (2013) *The National Curriculum in England: Framework Document.* London: DfE.

Index